STEPHEN PEARCE

WARRIOR SPIRIT

Written at the Kitchen Table

the old-fashioned way.

I can hardly believe all of this happened

to me.

For every book sold a contribution will be made to COPE
Foundation towards creating a more fulfilled future for
Down's syndrome.

Published by Spirit Design Ltd.

Printed in Italy by TAP GRAFICHE s.r.l.

ISBN: 978-0-9926418-0-1
Limited Edition ISBN: 978-0-9926418-1-8

STEPHENPEARCE●COM

Opposite: Stephen Pearce. Photo Elliott Erwitt (he preferred the totem to my face).

"The story of Stephen Pearce is an important part of the story of modern Irish design."

Barbara Dawson, Director of Dublin City Gallery The Hugh Lane

"Nobody has had more influence on high quality design in the Irish household
 over the past 100 years than Stephen Pearce."

Paul Hogan, co-founder of Kilkenny Design Workshops

"Philip Pearce and his sons are part of the rock on which modern Irish design is built."

Michael Scott, Architect

INDEX:

FOREWORD

I bought my first piece of Shanagarry pottery in 1967 in a craft shop in Letterkenny on a hitchhiking trip in Co. Donegal. It was a little jug, a present for my Mum... actually it was a peace offering because it was supposed to be a cycling holiday but we dumped the bikes and hitchhiked instead! I loved the pottery but had no idea where Shanagarry was.

When I came to Ballymaloe to work in the kitchens several years later, I discovered that the little village of Shanagarry was just two miles away. As soon as I got my first pay packet of £4.50 I cycled over to find the Pottery. I found a kindly potter – Stephen's father Philip – who I think was intrigued and bemused by this young girl who was determined to spend her first week's wages on pottery. He mentioned that his sons Stephen and Simon were away; Stephen was in Japan studying with a master potter, and Simon in New Zealand with another potter. There was a flurry of excitement soon after when Stephen arrived home. I met this tall, gangly, flamboyant, zanily dressed chap. He was like no one I had ever met before: unpredictable, outrageous, impulsive and crazily creative. He hopped on the potter's wheel and started to turn out a whole new range of pots, everything from jugs and mugs to totem poles. I've always regretted not buying one of Steve's totem poles, but I did buy many of his special pots including a bread crock which he really didn't want to sell. I pleaded so much that eventually he relented and said, "Right, I'll sell it for £15." Over three weeks wages! Oops. He didn't expect me to say yes. The bread crock is still one of my treasured possessions.

Darina Allen, 4th February 2013

A TRIBUTE
TO KEVIN
DUNNE

This book was conceived as a tribute to my dear friend Kevin Dunne, the incredibly talented photographer who took all my pictures for nearly forty years. We first met when he came to my father's Pottery in 1969 to take what he called a 'photie' for that year's Bank of Ireland calendar. We hit it off immediately. He was staying in Ballymaloe so we headed out for supper and a long night of talk and tomfoolery ensued. Kevin had managed the Greenbeats, the first really successful Irish four piece band. I was totally into music. I had sung Elvis songs with the school band and was into American Blues and was fascinated with the British music scene that was developing at the time.

Next year Kevin was back to photograph Francesca, my first wife, making batiks this time for Esso. For devilment someone had put a marijuana plant in the shot. When Victor the art director was making the presentation to Esso someone pointed out that, as a major US company, they wouldn't have a sense of humour about the plant. So Victor changed the colour register to make the plant a brown colour and nobody noticed. Kevin and I were cast in the same mould. As a professional photographer he always wanted to do his very best work. After a few sessions I told him, "Stop asking me what I want and just do it."

One reason Kevin's photos of my pots work for me, is because they are as much the pots as the pots themselves. Neither photo nor pots steal the limelight. They sit very easily together, which is what I like my pots to do. Over the years, Kevin managed to sneak the pots into all sorts of ads and so we made sure he always had a serious stash of them in his studio. When Kevin wanted help styling a shot he would get his wife Isabel to set it up. At one stage Isabel had a flower shop called the Egg Depot which was great because she could choose precisely the flowers that she needed. Kevin was over the moon when his second daughter Sally became a professional photography stylist. She is now one of the best in Dublin and had a hand in many of our photos. Kevin and I had always intended doing a book of houses that I have worked on, and in fact, we had begun to shoot a pilot for it. Unfortunately, time ran out on Kevin. His loyalty as a friend and his professionalism were a source of tremendous comfort and pleasure to me. I had Kevin keep all of the negatives and trannies so whenever a magazine needed something they could choose from a huge collection of shots. All the pictures on the Pottery walls were printed by his friend Neasa. They are more than just prints, they are art. I don't think Kevin had any idea how good a photographer he was. He was a bit like me. We just do what we are doing to the best we can and leave it to you to judge. We always lived at such a pace that there was never time for retrospection. We were always off here, there and somewhere else, busy working on the next project. If there is a next life I bet Kevin is there with a grin from ear to ear saying, "Now that I'm gone who'll you get to do the photies?" and he's right. When Isabel and I went to Kevin's filing cabinet we found 7,500 shots of my pots and family. Vanessa O'Reilly put them all on high resolution discs and my wife Lauren spent months choosing the shots for this book. It was one of the most difficult parts of putting this book together as each and every one of Kevin's 7,500 photos is beautiful and warrants inclusion.

INTRODUCTION

"Welcome to my book. Don't forget to read all the words."
Stephen Pearce

I love communicating. I never meant to be a potter; I wanted to be a rock singer. After a few years in the rock'n'roll business in London I realised that not only did I like making pottery with my father but that it could be my launch pad for performing and communicating with lots of people. Pottery is under my skin, but like many artists I find it impossible to rate my work. All I know is that I have given it my all and that I am passionate about what I do. If you are reading this it means that I have a friend somewhere. Thanks.

The initial stimulus for this book was to honour my dear friend Kevin Dunne, the photographer who took most of the pictures you'll see. Secondly I wanted to share with my children and you what a demanding and exciting life I have led with the main focus on my father's and my Pottery. As I have a friendship with many Pottery customers I thought that you might like to know some of the effort and madness that has gone into my life, what it felt like to crash on my face when I lost the Pottery in 2008 and the struggle to get back in the game. The idea of this book is to tell the story of our family Pottery as experienced by me, including some of the lessons I have picked up on the way.

It was easy and enjoyable writing the first draft. Then it got strange. I began to see myself and what I had done from your point of view. I particularly felt the pain that my mother and brother must have felt at the way I was at times. So much of what went on during my life happened at such breakneck speed that my experience at the time was like having a business lunch in a smart restaurant while putting a deal together. I often walked out of great restaurants not having tasted a single bite. Now looking back I can live things as they happened and get the full flavour and emotional content. At first I judged myself pretty harshly and regretted many instances of not being open and sensitive to other people's needs. As I wrote on I began to see that given where I was at any time and with the experience available to me I mostly did the best I could, which makes me happy. It's nice to be nice to oneself.

As a designer my currency is ideas. I have found that if I allow an idea to become a belief it takes on an unmoveable solidity rather like constipation in my gut. Belief often takes the form of me believing that I am right. Hopefully I can catch myself in time, keep my ideas loose and playful and take an attitude of *what if?*

In tandem with hanging loose on ideas there is the ancient wisdom that says everything in the universe is interconnected as one stream of consciousness. What you are, so am I. What you feel and experience, so do I. The only difference is that your mind and my mind may interpret our experience differently, and therefore separately. When I play with this concept I notice all sorts of tendencies in my self that I usually just smooth over: fun and not so fun.

Take the analogy of a planet covered in metal bugs called cars. Each car thinks it is special. I am big, I am small, I am red, I am fast, I am strong, I am Japanese, I am French, I have sat nav, I have snow tyres. The truth is that until recently all had the same spiritual connection without which they would all be sitting rusting at the side of the road. Petrol. That is what they share in common and makes their world go round.

For us, it's this universal energy, without beginning and without end. So I am you and you are me. I know the religions have temporarily hijacked the need for us to hack our path through the forests of doubt, delusions and distractions to try and find ourselves, but go out and buy a machete today. There is lots of fun out in the forest.

Now you know where I am coming from with this book. I have lived an amazing and varied life and only realised it while writing for you, and realising that I was writing for me. I think the key to my exciting adventure was my mother and father supporting each other in putting no boundaries, obstacles or beliefs in my way. If they had, I have no idea whether I would have had the courage to carry on full tilt anyway. Maybe.

Kevin and I were friends for forty years, which is a book in itself. We were about the same age

but he died way before me. I decided to mark our friendship with this book. My wife worked through 7,500 images and we settled on 200. I wrote an introduction about Kevin and myself and decided that a very simple history of my father's Pottery was in order. It seemed rather dry so I started giving my feelings and ideas about how the Pottery evolved and developed. As I started writing I found my own self and story creeping in and realised that the only thing I could write about with real feeling was my own experience. So what you have is Kevin's photos, the history of the Pottery and what that whole journey has been like for me. You also have my observations on life which go beyond me and include you. Hence my spiel about us all being one. I see this as the key to our future.

S♣P

Note to the text: To avoid confusion I have drawn a distinction throughout the book between Pottery (capital 'P') when talking about the place where the pots are made, and pottery when referring to the pieces made there.

PART 1
FAMILY TREE

RUMOURS & REMINISCENCES

"Shanagarry, from old Gaelic Sean Gairdín 'Old Garden'."
Stephen Pearce

Two original Youghal vases circa 1910, decorated with household paint.

My original unfired money box made by Willie Greene 1952.

Photos Patrick Treacy

I have been told that there were Potteries stretching from Youghal town back up the Blackwater River and one of its estuaries for hundreds of years. Apparently, as you go upstream the quality of the earthenware clay improves and so is less likely to chip and crack; all of the things that pottery naturally does and which we potters constantly fight against.

Just outside Youghal there is a brick factory from the last century, while two miles upriver at Curraghboy, where I dig my clay every summer, there still exists an old kiln from the 1800s that produced household pottery into the 20th century.

Willie Greene, of one of the long-time pottery families, proudly took my father to this very field in 1952, recalling that his father swore that the best clay in Youghal was to be found there and that three generations of his family had worked in the Pottery making milk and water jugs. Wide shallow bowls were made to hold milk so the cream could rise to the top and later be skimmed off with a thin wooden plate made of sycamore. There were large urns for storing fish and salt pork, as well as flower vases. For the tourists of the day, who would arrive in Youghal from Cork on a Sunday jaunt by train or for a short holiday, there were souvenirs: money boxes for the children, flower baskets as ornaments and small cream jugs to put on the dresser and be prized. Sometimes people would paint the pots with house paint. I have a couple of these on a shelf at our Pottery still. Of course the money box had to be broken for the money to be retrieved and I always looked forward to that day. The thought of a stash of hard-saved loot sparkling in front of my eyes, especially the brown pennies with all the different animals that Irish coins had on them in those days, would make me feel very excited as well as knowing that the three ten bob notes that I had been given by my godmother would be in there. I still have the first money box that Willie gave me even before we had a kiln to fire it in. He baked it in the Aga cooker; a tip I still give to children to this day. For some reason I never cracked that first money box. Maybe I was too attached to it. I can still smell the clay and see Willie with his nicotine stained fingers and the grapes growing overhead in the greenhouse at Ballymaloe where we were living and where the first pots were made. Imagine my joy at recently finding this, one of my favourite pots, after almost sixty years. I quickly shook it, but nothing. Someone else must have bought those thin slivers of Dairy Milk bars, gob stoppers and sherbet bags with the liquorice straw I dreamt of. I would hate to think all that money, maybe ten or fifteen euros worth, wasn't spent on sweets.

Willie used to tell me stories (I was about nine at the time), about how boats would come over from Wales with coal for the kilns and then load up with pottery for merchants in the UK (which also made good ballast for the return journey) up until 1920. He told me about the brickworks down the road, where a whole caravan of flat carts would pull in to be loaded by hand and leave in the afternoon. The men would sleep as the carts moved slowly along the road with the bricks to build terraces in Cork city. The lead horse knew the road and the other carts just followed along. The men would wake up when the caravan stopped in Carrigtwohill for breakfast before continuing to Cork to unload and then turn around once more.

Willie told me about his grandfather who well into his seventies would bend deep into a forty-five gallon drum to scrape galena from the bottom of the barrel so as not to waste any of the precious glaze material. Willie said his grandfather would come out coughing and cursing and spit out the dust before going back into the barrel. He must have been a mighty man as galena was the forerunner of red lead and far more toxic. It did however produce an amazing and brilliant glaze when mixed with some liquid clay. We had to stop using galena in the early 1960s and move on to red lead. Then later we had to stop using red lead and only use fluxes that are baked with other materials so that they cannot leach out during use. It was the right move. A paint factory and ourselves had to stop using it because unfortunately some ingenious child in England had died from eating the paint off a staircase banister. It sounds just like the sort of thing I would have done. Today pottery containing lead and fired at very low temperatures still comes in from Mexico, Spain, Portugal and North Africa. You know you are in for a lead cocktail when acidic fruit like raspberries or lemons, or vinegar start to fizz immediately in a low-fired pot.

The first time that I went to the clay field I was about ten. Every year the men would take about six inches of top soil off a space about ten feet wide by fifteen feet long. The chosen space was always ordained by Willie as having the finest clay. Willie was about eighty at the time and so did very little digging. He usually chose a place under gorse bushes for us to dig, though I am sure he did that just to blackguard the others and give them the trouble of clearing the gorse. Willie always insisted that my father bring an ample supply of pint bottles of Guinness and, by 10am, would be sitting in the shade with his first pint giving orders. Digging clay was hard work. Any bit of rain and it stuck to the shovels. No rain and it was hard as the hobs of hell.

My father had an old beat-up Land Rover and we would all pile in with shovels, picks, food hampers and booze. He quickly learned not to take too much booze as Willie would be very cantankerous by mid-afternoon. We'd all be hoping that he'd fall asleep and not be annoying us. By the age of fourteen, I took my pick (a grufán actually as it had a wider blade to slice the clay) and sweated it out with Mick Donovan, Timmy O'Keefe and Patsy Fahey. I learned a lot from those men: how to start the day nice and easy and be up to speed by ten o'clock and then hold that pace all day. We would spread the sods of clay over the grass for a day or two to dry and then fill the back of the jeep and take it the half mile out to the road.

Apart from the 'blind doctors' (horse flies, so called because they gave you a pick like a doctor's injection), the clay field at Curraghboy was a magical place. A rough, hilly field with a strong feeling of history and the old derelict Pottery with its bottle kiln where we would shelter on the wet days. The river where the cattle stood for hours cooling down and where I would go for a dip myself on hot days; it was a lazy, easy romantic place where hard work and blackguarding took place and great stories were told.

Mr Ducey, to whom we paid £20 a year to dig our pit, had an ancient tractor run on TVO (pre-diesel Tractor Vaporising Oil). He started it by swinging a crank in front and if it kicked the wrong way he would have three reverse gears and one forward. Then he would just drive it that way. I would hear and meet him coming around a bush backwards. He always stopped to chat. I asked him one day why he drove the tractor backwards and he said, "Sure any fool could drive a tractor forwards." The tractor never did any work, he was just very proud to be one of the first small farmers to own one. He was forever inviting me back to his little thatched farmhouse for tea and freshly made soda bread. I'll never forget the smell of the turf fire and the soda bread, freshly-baked in the bastible, with lots of farm butter and homemade jam. At that time, the older people in Ireland tipped the hot tea from their cup, which usually had lots of sugar in it, into the saucer to cool and then drank the tea from the saucer. Another quaint habit was that people, having cut up their lunch, would eat from their knife rather than the fork.

Above: In the door of the 19th century bottle kiln at the clay field.

Opposite: We dig our clay late summer so that the ground is hard enough for heavy lorries. A US magazine needed a photo of digging clay in February. So Tom Shinnick got out his wheelbarrow and I put on my Davy Crockett hat!

When we had two loads of clay out by the road, a lorry would come and we would shovel the clay into the lorry and back at home we would shovel it off again. There were no tipping lorries in those days. I once counted that there were eighteen hand processes in preparing the clay before it even reached the potter's wheel.

By the mid-1960s, the JCB had arrived. God bless the man who invented that machine. The first JCB we hired was second hand and kept bursting oil pipes with the strain of digging our clay. As Mick Donovan said to me one day, "Weren't we mighty men to do that work by hand?" to which Patsy Fahey replied, "Sure we knew no better."

After we unloaded the raw clay from Youghal with its stones and gorse bushes, it had to sit on a concrete slab for at least a year to gain more plasticity so that it would be better for throwing. The clay would then be barrowed into an open shed where it would be spread out to dry. Years later came the HyMac and huge tipping

*John Walsh loads raw clay into the Wash Mill.
Stones will be washed out and a thick cream
will be sieved ready to be squeezed dry by the
Filter Press.*

lorries. Now we can dig a hundred and fifty tons in a day instead of thirty tons in two weeks.

As the clay dried it was broken down finer and finer and the stones were picked out. Finally the clay was pounded to dust with a sledgehammer and loaded into forty-five gallon barrels which were half full of water. I then mixed the clay and water to a thick, creamy consistency by hand using a special homemade tool. I loved doing this work as it built up my muscles for rugby in the autumn. And I could show off to the girls, (yes, we are still cavemen – and women).

When the clay reached the right consistency it was sieved and put into troughs made from low-fired clay tiles which absorbed the moisture. Once it reached the consistency of bread dough, we took handfuls and put it on pottery boards to dry further. Next it was taken to a well-insulated clay store and put through a pug mill. The pug mill is a bit like a mincing machine with a single

John Walsh and Tom Shinnick drop cakes of stiff clay from the Filter Press ready for the Pug Mill.

Paddy Fitz taking a sausage of clay from the Pug Mill to be stored for six months. The shelves were made from old billiards tables.

hole at one end. The clay is mixed and extruded in 4-inch diameter sausages and then stored to mature in a cellar-like atmosphere. Nowadays, although all the basic principles still apply, our process is much more mechanised with the star of the show being a machine for mixing the raw clay so that I don't have to stir barrels forever.

I recall in the late 1960s I was given the job of visiting Dominick Smiddy to agree a price for the clay, as he had bought the farm from the Ducey family. It was always a pleasure dealing with Dominick and his wife Cora. There was no argument and I always got a great breakfast and was sorry to leave their company. One day I was just saying goodbye on the doorstep of their house when I looked at the three young daughters and said to Dominick, "I suppose I should buy an acre of the clay field." "Why?" says Dominick, "It is far easier on your pocket to just pay

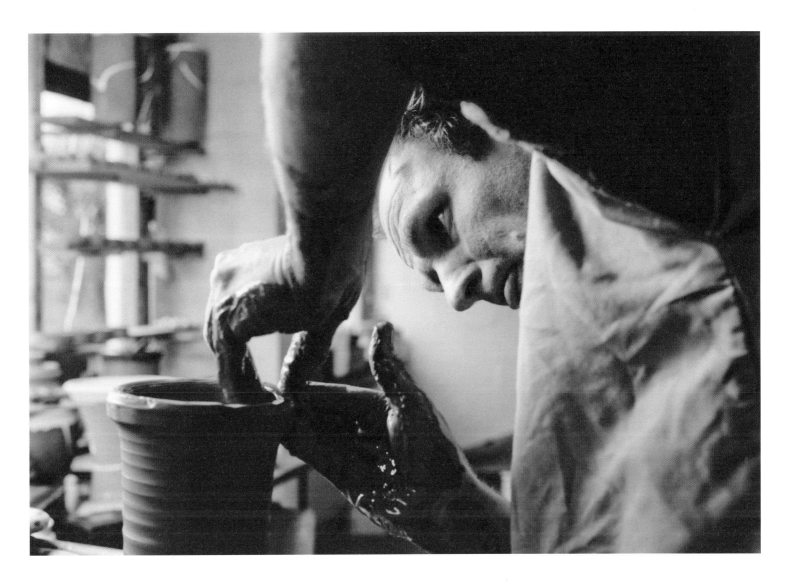

for what you take." I replied, "Please don't be insulted, as it's nothing to do with your family. But, say one of the three girls marries a cute fella who realises that without clay I am banjaxed, then I am helpless." Dominick, as a farmer and cattle dealer, immediately saw my point and sold me five acres at a very fair price. As a result we now have enough clay for many generations. It costs us more to dig and prepare our own clay than to import a ready to use clay from England, however, historically pottery has always been made near the clay source, or the coal source or the forest for fuel. It's always been about the transport costs of heavy raw materials. For this reason Britain and Europe had Potteries and steel works close to canals.

The clay at Youghal is a very high quality and unique deposit and makes a pottery that is far more durable than many earthenware clays. When I make pots I sense the clay field and I remember Willie Greene and all that went before him. Our pottery is very much of the place. I cannot imagine using a clay that I don't prepare myself. When there is a problem with the quality of the clay, as there is from time to time, having prepared the clay ourselves it is usually obvious what is wrong and we can then run it through the preparation process again to remedy the problem. Clay is an organic living material and needs to mature like wine for as long as six months. As with wine, it can pass its 'best before' date and has to be reprocessed all over again.

For me, making pots is the clay that I use. I very much enjoy our clay and, as I've said, when I put a piece of Youghal clay

Above: The second process in making a pot is the lifting of a hollow cylinder from the lump of clay on the wheel. This requires muscle.

Opposite: (clockwise from top left) Continuing to lift the cylinder. Putting finishing touches to a honey jar. Pouring and directing the glaze.

Nora Paul decorating.

Piaras Kelly glazing.

on the wheel I am instantly linked to history, Willie Greene, the gorse bushes, the smell of the clay and its plasticity which I have gained through careful preparation and storage. Occasionally when the clay isn't quite right there are a lot of F words.

The secret to making pottery by hand on a potter's wheel is to get the wobbledy, slippery piece of clay in the centre of the wheel. This is not something that I can decide to do with my mind. As with riding a bicycle, through practice I arrived at a point where my hand, eye and brain were all coordinated and a miracle happened. I stopped struggling with the sloppy lump of clay. After centring there was a set of mini-skills which I acquired one by one over a number of years. An apprenticeship used to take five years. I think after two years there should be a few saleable pots. However larger and more intricate pots do take a lot of time and patience. Making pottery takes discipline. Everything – working surfaces, pottery boards, sponges – in the making and glazing needs to be spotlessly clean. From the moment a pot is made it needs to be minded. First turning it upside down when the rim begins to dry; then if a handle is needed, both handle and pot need to be united at the correct moment. For the first firing everything needs to be completely dry, particularly plates. When there is a rush on this is particularly important. I have occasionally taken a stack of six dinner plates or large curly bowls out of a bisque kiln with every one cracked across the base.

Glaze must be constantly mixed and sieved for consistency, removing lumps and foreign crap. Placing glazed pots in the right part of a kiln, for temperature, without chipping glaze or having two pieces touching is a great skill. Another great skill is grading our pottery; as with individually handmade pots there are always slight differences between pieces. However it is possible, if there is a temperature difference between two dinner plates in a kiln, that one may turn out a quarter inch smaller than the other. They are both perfect but one ends up as a second. All of our seconds are seconds for technical reasons that don't affect their life expectancy. It's rather like trying to organise an unruly crowd.

Not having dug clay for the past five years as the Pottery was closed, I went to pay my respects to Dominick and Cora in 2012. It is more than fifty years since I bought the field from Dominick. He is in his eighties and I find him out hunting in the cows and as bright as a button. I was telling him how, when my father sent me down to him the first time to do the deal for the clay, my father's instructions were to pay him what he asked and not to be arguing. Dominick, who has spent his life dealing in cattle, looked me straight in the eye with a big grin and said, "That was poor advice." I replied, "I didn't stay that innocent for long." §✤P

MY MOTHER, LUCY HELEN CROCKER

"Intelligence is being able to see what is right in front of your nose."
Lucy Pearce

B orn in 1901, my mother Lucy Helen Crocker had roots in the mining villages of south Wales. All her family before her father were miners who died of coal dust in their early forties. My grandfather, Alfie Crocker, moved from the mines to work on the Cardiff docks. I have always fantasised that he worked in a little wooden box office handing out dockets to merchants who came to collect coal. What is certain is that he was an office worker. A dapper little man with tight-cropped, curly, white hair, he was always well groomed. On camping holidays Alfie would wear a tweed waistcoat and long socks up to his knees outside his trousers. Emotions were probably not high on his agenda, except when I called in to collect a few bits and pieces that my grandmother had willed to my mother. The poor man had totally fallen apart and I couldn't bear to stay the night. He brought out a pot of plum jam for our tea that Granny had made and the tears proceeded to fall heavy down his cheeks. It's strange how men often wait until the one they love has gone before they really realise how much they loved them and how to fully express that emotion. We men must try to do better, both for ourselves and for the people we love.

My maternal grandmother was a formidable little woman but very kind and lov-

Above: Granny Crocker holding her eldest daughter Lucy circa 1902.

Below (left to right): Alfie standing with stick, Lucy sitting and Granny. Taken while enjoying a holiday outing.

Left to right: Sister Freda, Granny, sister Betty and Lucy. Probably outside their Cardiff home.

ing to my brother Simon and myself. My grandfather's small timber garage always smelled strongly of creosote, which I loved as it put me in mind of building and new fencing posts. Around the little black Ford car were stacked tents, lawn mowers and garden tools. Just outside the door was a huge purple lilac tree and I will never forget the perfume of lilac mixed with the smell of creosote.

They lived in a Victorian terraced house in Cardiff, and when the milkman delivered the glass milk bottles Granny would order different cordials for Simon and I. She was very strict about how much cordial we used in a glass of water. Coming from rural Shanagarry, the big thrills for us were the playground with swings just down the road and the black and white television showing Bill & Ben the Flowerpot Men. In the mornings, I would empty my hot water bottle into the bathroom sink to wash my face as the hot water was only switched on once a week for baths and for washing clothes by hand. I can still remember how the water smelled of rubber from the bottle. What Granny didn't know was that I never washed my face at home in Ireland.

My mother Lucy was the eldest of three sisters, Betty and Freda being the younger ones. Lucy was sent to university but there was no money to send Betty or Freda. My mother did well academically and became one of the first female university professors in Britain. She was involved in the Suffragette Movement and the starting of the Youth Hostel Movement, which is where she met my father.

My mother's subject and special interest was biology, which she soon turned into human biology and the study of human behaviour. In 1935 Lucy and a group of like-minded doctors, sociologists and an organic farmer, started a project in Peckham on the edge of London, called the Peckham Experiment. At a time when researchers all over the world were beginning to focus on disease and specific cures for every illness, my mother and her gang decided to look at the conditions in which health was most likely to flourish.

At that time in England there were a good number of successful industrialists who wanted to put a share of their profits back in to the advancement of a broader society. The Peckham Experiment was fortunate in capturing the interest of several such philanthropists. An ultra modern building was constructed. It was simply four concrete platforms with glass walls inside and out. At a time when most institutional buildings were short on natural light, the Peckham gang were strong on sunlight for people and vegetables. It was 1935,

and being in a poor area at the time meant the range of food was limited and lacked nutritional value. The vision and possibilities for the people living in Peckham were also very limited, so naturally there was a lot of suspicious curiosity around this very unusual building with no walls, erected in a large open field against the backdrop of an urban setting.

The concept of the Peckham Experiment was to have a club, which only the entire family could join, with activities for every member of the family. There was a huge three-storey gym with ropes and two indoor heated swimming pools and a large asphalt apron at the front of the building with bicycles and roller skates, as well as air raid shelters where the older boys and girls went to smoke and kiss. The mothers had all sorts of adult education classes including sewing and learning about organic food and how to cook it. The men played billiards, learned to read, made sets for plays and did repairs. The idea of the glass walls was that the whole family could see what the others were up to, and in so doing get conversations going back at home. With improved communication and a level of family intimacy came dramatically improved health.

I was there as a young child of five. We kids had lots of Montessori toys and a young Australian minder called Elizabeth Neave. Elizabeth was a close friend of my mother's and really got us kids in a way most people didn't, and still don't. We used to sit on the floor by those huge glass windows and look out. Years

Above: The Peckham building.

Below: The gym and swimming pool in the Peckham building.

after Peckham, she came to Ireland and joined Shanagarry Pottery. As my father aged, Elizabeth took on the running of his Pottery, and many people still think that Elizabeth is my mother.

My mother knew Maria Montessori and was a great fan of hers. She loved experimentation, something she instilled in us at home and which was also evidenced by her undertakings in Peckham. Maria saw the purpose of her equipment as a rational process to develop the intellect. My mother saw the added possibility of letting us play with the equipment and finding new ways to develop our own uses for it, something Maria would have disagreed with. My mother was way ahead of her time in her openness to the world and she saw the process of life and creation as a limitless work in progress. She was determined that her children should participate as fully as possible in this joyful journey of exploration and discovery.

The top floor of the centre in Peckham was given over to doctors, researchers and medical staff. Once a month, the whole family went for a check up and discussion. One of the more unusual concepts of the time at Peckham was my mother's idea that there is no separation that we can distinguish between our physical and mental or emotional being. She felt that to try to separate the two is to miss the point of being human, the two being totally interrelated and integrated. For example, is stress physical or mental? I would suggest that it is a chicken and egg scenario. This was the beginning of the age of 'meatball science': the idea that if you keep chopping matter to smaller components, you eventually arrive at the basic building block of creation. Well it still hasn't happened and I suppose the basic unit, if there is one, is possibly more than physical, and so the possibilities are limitless. With this over-complication of science, sometimes the simple realities of life get sidelined. Something I find extraordinary is that given what an exciting game life is, how few people allow themselves to join in, in a full and meaningful way.

In Peckham, as with any urban area that had sacrificed its men and women to World War I, there was a real sense of social confusion that led to chaos within families and resulted in all sorts of stress. For this reason, the Peckham Experiment focused on the family as the unit rather than the individual. You could argue the wisdom of this forever. However, the context for the study was for families that had been separated for a number of years by the war. I remember hearing that all too often during the war either or both parents may have found love outside the family. Children may have been the offspring of one parent only. There may also have been children from the marriage. Wives, who had got used to managing on their own, found themselves with a man in the house who either couldn't find work or was having difficulty adjusting to ordinary life again. Imagine several children running around the house. The husband is sitting at the table reading the newspaper. The wife places an uninteresting plate of food under the paper. Nothing is said. Neither has anything to say. He resents the boring food and feels useless for not being able to provide for his family. She wishes she could provide better and resents him for not saying thank you. He probably pushes half the food away and goes to the pub. When he gets back he may feel like sex. What does she do? Well it depends whether he is violent or not. These sorts of family breakdowns are very common after wars, which is why my mother and her colleagues wanted to bring communication back into families.

During World War II, The Centre (as it was called) became an ammunitions factory. Once it had re-opened after the war, I went there with my brother in 1948 and we lived in a house next door. In our yard there were a couple of old army tanks. Guess where Simon and I played? My brother and I each had mugs made by the English potter Harry Davis. One had a little squiggly motorbike racing around it and the other a car. There was war if either of us took the wrong mug, which of course we often did. There were a lot of old ammunition cases at The Centre which my mother got for us to take apart. They were beautifully made for all sorts of fancy equipment. When I dismantled the cases, I built many different carts and houses with them. Organic food, kids running around naked and barefoot: this was the order of the day. My mother was stopped several times in Harrods department store by the RSPCC for cruelty to children because of my bare feet. I remember on Shanagarry strand when I was five years old a bevy of nuns came past as I ran around naked and one of them said, "Look. He's like a little nigger!" S☘P

*Left to right: Lucy in Wilson Strangman's garden (now Tim and Darina Allen's Cookery School);
Lucy at the shooting of* Moby Dick *on the quayside in Youghal.*

MY FATHER, PHILIP WALTER PEARCE

"I have a dream."
  Martin Luther King, Jr.

Philip with his mother.

Walter Pearce, my paternal grandfather, was a merchant craftsman from Cornwall who went to London and started his own printing press. He came from a long line of Methodist ministers, the first of whom was converted by Charles Wesley. My father Philip was born in 1911. The eldest of two boys, his mother May died before he was six. Walter lived in a town house in Brentford Middlesex which had a large garden and a coach house. The printing press, which employed about twelve people, was across the 'Butts', a piece of land that had been used since the 16th century for archery practice that sloped from the house to the printing works.

Philip was an unusual man. A very gentle soul who didn't fit most male stereotypes, he went to a lesser English Public School, as befitted a merchant craftsman's son in the early 1920s. Of course, being a British school there was an army officer training corps for the sons of the Empire. My father was a young man of conscience and could not countenance the notion of one human deliberately killing another. I think he would be happy that I and my son Oran both agree with him on this count. At school, whenever the other boys went to practice war games, my father would take his portable wind-up gramophone and find a hiding place to listen to classical music. A shy man, he was also interested in meditation and Sufism.

Having studied at the London School of Printing, he worked with Walter in the printing press and also ran a high quality, second hand rare and antiquarian bookstore called The Beauchamp Bookshop. When Philip was young, the household coachman turned up with his twelve year old daughter Lily who started helping in the kitchen. Lily Flatt stayed with our family all her life. She came to Ireland for many years and then in her seventies went back to London to take care of Philip's aunt Emily Lobb (née Stallibrass). Both died in the same nursing home aged over ninety.

In the late 1930s Walter traded in his horses and carriage for an Alvis motor car. It was like a lesser Rolls Royce. Meanwhile Philip, in a very simple way, restored the loft over the coach house as his flat. Shortly after this he joined the London Ambulance Service as a dispatch rider and he and his father trained to do night work watching for incendiary bombs.

With the shadow of war approaching, Philip, aged almost thirty, a trained printer, ambulance driver and fireman, was summoned to join the army. He told the officer that he would not carry a gun but that he would work on ambulances or fire engines. He was told to return the next day to go to jail. He got on his bicycle and cycled from London to Fishguard from where he sailed to Cork. The next day an architect friend of his in Cork took him to Quaker Meeting where he met Ivan Allen. After the Meeting, Ivan invited Philip to lunch in Shanagarry and that night they stayed up talking until the early hours of the morning. Philip and Ivan were complete opposites but their ensuing long, close friendship was based on mutual respect for the gifts the other had.

Ivan lived in a newly built house in Shanagarry. His family were from Drogheda where they had a cotton mill making towels. At school, a bit like myself, Ivan had been good at carpentry. After he finished school, Wilson Strangman, who lived with his sister Lydia in Kinoith in Shanagarry (where Tim and Darina Allen established Ballymaloe Cookery School), invited Ivan to Shanagarry to come and try to make sense of his farm. Wilson was a gentle soul but not very practical. One of Ivan's first projects was to plant apple trees and call it 'Imokilly Orchards' as it was in the barony of Imokilly. Then followed tomatoes and mushrooms before he bought Ballymaloe and became involved in dairy and pig farming; all prior to his wife Myrtle opening her Yeats Room restaurant in 1964. Philip being a typographer and printer designed the labels and stationery for Imokilly Orchards.

When Philip arrived in Shanagarry, he checked into Ardnahinch, the Motherways' pub and farmhouse right on the edge of the cliffs of Shanagarry strand. Freda Motherway put my father up, fed him and did his washing for twelve shillings a week. Seventy-two years later two of her grandnieces, Carrie and Helen, are here with me in the Pottery.

My parents had been involved for a number of years in setting up the Youth Hostel Association in England. Lucy was eight years Philip's senior and a very organised person, unlike Philip who was quite easy going. At this stage Lucy and Philip were just friends and as they lived quite close by in London, Philip would often drive Lucy to the YHA meetings where everyone would talk themselves into a knot while Lucy, who was a headmistress of a 600-pupil girl's school in west London, would sit quietly knitting. Eventually, she would put down her knitting, stand up and say, "Thank you all very much for your valuable contributions. Now, this is what I want you to do before the next meeting", and she would give everyone a task. It must have been quite extraordinary having this coalminer's daughter, in her long woolly socks and heavy glasses, with her powerful intellect cutting through the bullshit that all of these important and wealthy people were talking. At a meeting in Liverpool, a group of Irish lads arrived over with the idea of starting youth hostels in Ireland. My mother used to say that they were led by the "extremely handsome" Terry Trench, the father of Fiacra and Brian, both of whom became good friends of mine some twenty years later.

As Lucy and Philip drove to their meetings, Philip being in his late-twenties and Lucy in her mid-thirties, she would chide him for not getting married. In a very nice way, Lucy always took control, not because she was controlling but, like me, she liked to see things get done. As Philip wasn't getting it together himself to get married, in around 1937 Lucy fixed him up with Pam, her favourite ex-pupil. It worked and they planned to get married despite Philip's move to Shanagarry soon after.

Cycling home from work with Ivan at the Orchards Philip fell in love with one of Ivan's fields looking over Ballycotton Bay. Ivan allowed him to build a small bungalow there which Philip called the White

Above (left to right): Philip as curious as ever with Ivan and Myrtle Allen inspecting the field for the White House. Below: The newly finished White House facing south over Ballycotton Bay and about 100m from the shoreline.

House. Ivan paid for the materials and owned the house. It was a very modern house for its time with simple interiors and a huge picture window looking out onto the beach. Patrick Scott, the artist and architect, later designed an extension (maybe a space for when I arrive!) I suspect that it was in return for this kindness of Ivan's that Philip later borrowed money from his father to help Ivan buy Ballymaloe.

Before long disaster struck and Pam died of tuberculosis in London before they were due to be married. Philip then wrote to Lucy and asked her to marry him. Lucy, not being an impetuous person said she needed some time to think about it. Philip replied, "Just come over, I know it will be alright." She flew to Dublin and the first time they kissed was when she arrived in Ireland. In her late thirties, Lucy was anxious to start having what she hoped would be a large family. A very successful career woman, she quit her job and committees because she felt that despite having spent her life thus far fighting for a woman's right to work, the most important and fulfilling thing that a woman can do is to raise and support a family. She wanted to have the time and space to enjoy and explore the experience fully. In a way our family was her laboratory. It was great. One of her achievements was to become an ace cook and when Myrtle was ready to start her restaurant, Lucy had the know-how to pass on.

Lucy and Philip were married in Cloyne Cathedral on 11th January 1942 and Wilson Strangman gave my mother away as her parents, being cautious, didn't want to cross the sea from Wales during the war. The honeymoon was at Molly Lyons' cottage in Glenbeigh. Ivan lent the honeymoon couple his huge old Ford – one of the very few motor cars in east Cork – which had been converted to steam due to wartime rationing of petrol, and which had a trailer behind with a steam boiler that had to be stoked with turf. After two weeks of sitting by Molly's fire, eating fresh soda bread and wandering the cliffs and beaches of Glenbeigh, the postman arrived on his bicycle with a telegram from Ivan wondering when he might get his car back.

An interesting piece of history is that while my father was working with Ivan Allen designing notepaper and lids for tomato and mushroom cartons in the late 1930s, my mother introduced him to Jack B. Yeats. Philip, at the age of thirty, still hadn't sorted out a career. Lucy could see that Philip had a creative eye and that while he was not commercially minded he had a strong artistic, creative side to everything he did. He went up to Dublin a number of times and he and Jack would paint together. One day, Jack said to Philip, "I don't think you are a painter but you have a great eye. Come to Dublin and I will hang some of my latest paintings on the wall and we can talk about them." I think it was on a Tuesday that he went when once a week Jack would have pals around for drinks or tea. At the end of the evening Jack said to my father, "You know these paintings are going to be very valuable some day". Philip told me that Jack was really sure of the monetary value of his work. Philip came back to Shanagarry and spoke to Ivan Allen, who was making good money selling tomatoes to war-torn Britain. Ivan gave Philip £600 to buy Yeats' paintings. Philip bought six paintings with the money including a large one of a blackbird bathing. When the deal was done, Jack felt that Philip should have a painting himself. This was from the heart. As a designer, and in life generally, I know how exciting it is when someone gets you and what you are about. Jack could see that Philip 'saw' his paintings and this made him happy. Philip returned with £40 and asked Jack to choose him something small. Jack chose *The Man in the Moon,* the only Yeats I've seen that crosses over slightly into abstract modern art. He also gave Philip a small painting for my mother as a gift. S&P

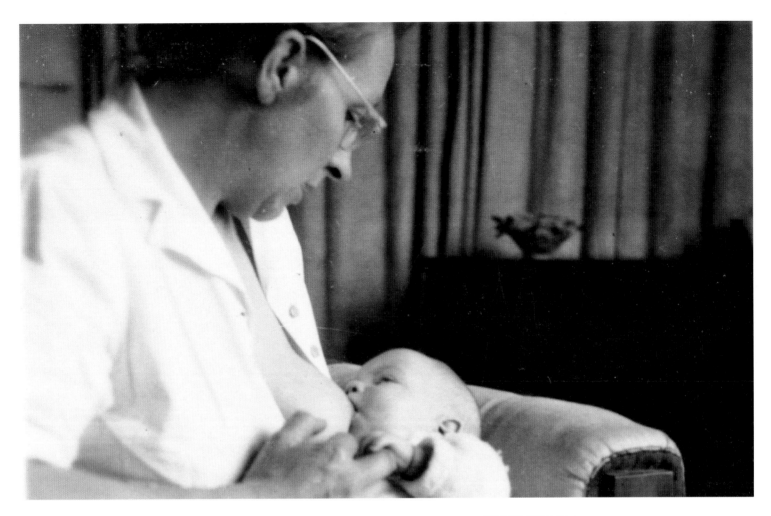

BEGINNINGS

"Welcome to this world (shit happens)".
Paolo Giorgini, Firenze circa 2006

I was conceived in Shanagarry in 1943. My mother had given birth the previous year to my older brother Andrew in Cork but the doctors squeezed the forceps too tightly and he died of brain damage two days later. Naturally my mother was distraught. At forty-one not only was her first child dead through carelessness, but I would now have to be born by caesarean section. As a result my mother had become so anti-Cork doctors that in December 1943 she sailed from Cork to Fishguard, through the German submarines lying in wait for American convoys bringing troops and supplies to Europe. I was delivered with the help of a dear friend of my mother's in the basement of Queen Charlotte's Hospital in London while bombs fell all around us. After two weeks under my grandfather's solid oak table we crossed over the submarines once more. For the same reason as before I never attended a Cork doctor until my mother died in 1974, when I was fortunate enough to meet Dr Catherine Molloy who became a very dear friend and was to save my life on three different occasions. I have since attended some great Cork doctors but I do understand my mother's reaction to her situation.

Top: Lucy making sure that I am well fed.
Above: Philip looking adoringly at me outside the White House gate.

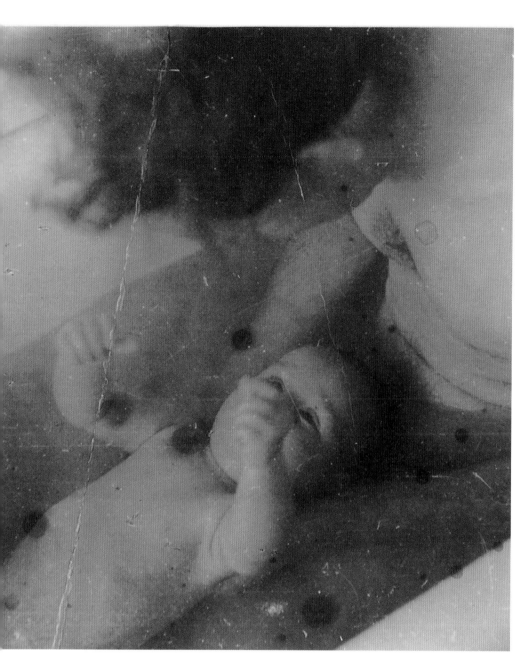

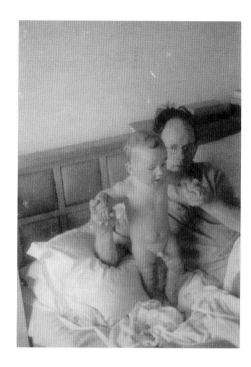

Three years later my mother gave birth to my brother Simon in London, also by caesarean section and finally, another three years later, she was able to have a natural birth for our sister Sarah. Sadly for my mother, Sarah was born with Down's syndrome. I use the word 'sadly' only because as someone whose whole life was about humans and having waited so long for a natural birth, I believe my mother felt guilty that Sarah had Down's. She loved her daughter dearly and put an incredible amount of energy into researching and doing the very best she could by Sarah. I always sensed however that my mother felt she had failed in some way, and that she had let the family down. I think this is a common feeling among women; part of the biology of child bearing and a woman's desire for what we have been taught is perfection. It is my experience that it is Nature's way of trying different possibilities. Our notion of beautiful, intelligent children is nonsense as we come in all shapes and sizes with our own intelligence. Sarah was welcomed into more homes in Shanagarry than any of us.

Prompted by Sarah's needs, Lucy was one of the founders, along with John Bermingham, of Cork Polio Aftercare Association, now called COPE, which has grown into a world-class organisation. My brother Simon and I are eternally grateful to the people of COPE for their support in helping us care for Sarah. As we travelled the world, it was great to have COPE as an anchor and to know that Sarah was being well looked after. At weekends Sarah would return to Shanagarry by bus and stay with Maureen Walsh whom she called "Ma" as Maureen was definitely a second mother to Sarah. Sarah died at fifty-five at COPE and was beautifully laid out by the staff but I couldn't bear to go into the room.

My early life was very free, going everywhere barefoot and often naked. Lucy never got over losing her first child and this meant she was deeply protective of me. We formed a powerful bond, which is still there today. The downside was that while she encouraged me to explore life, I knew that if anything happened to

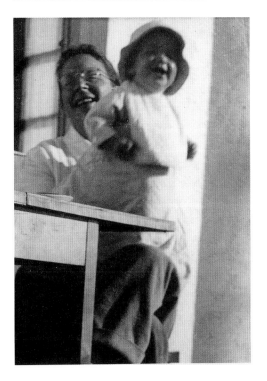

me she would never forgive herself. My reaction to this was to be quite rude and unkind to her at times as I saw her as being constantly on my case.

Right from the beginning I was surrounded by handmade objects of good design. At Shanagarry all my Montessori equipment was made by local carpenters. My shovels for digging in the sand were made by Dick Kennefick, Shanagarry's blacksmith. My coats were woven nearby in Knockadoon. Jumpers were knitted by my minder Katie Walsh. My mother made my little bed covers. Paddy Daly (known as Paddy Saddler because he made all of the tackle for the local carthorses) made my carrycot. And on it went. My first raincoat was made by my mother from a barrage balloon that had drifted across from England and landed on Shanagarry strand. All our marmalade in the winter of 1944 came from grapefruit and oranges washed ashore from American ships sunk by the Germans off Ireland. Lucy soaked the oranges for days in buckets of well water to get rid of the salt. We had no electricity but I loved the candles and lamps. 'Bob the Painter' (whose real name was Roach) painted ordinary oil lamps white and put a gold line around them that made them seem so special. Paddy Higgins was often around with my father. They started keeping bees at Kilmahon just down the road where Philip and Lucy would make pottery fifteen years later. My high chair (which all of my children and grandchildren have also used) was made from driftwood by a man in Glenbeigh, Co. Kerry in 1940. He made it and all of the chairs in our kitchen with almost no tools in the wintertime. Every year a couple more chairs would arrive at Midleton railway station. Of course they were always different sizes, depending on the humour. My mother was very specific about the measurements of the high chair though. I made a copy for Simon's children in America many years later. Originally all the chairs had *súgán* seats (*súgán* is a rope of twisted hay used by farmers for chair seats and many other things). Eventually we replaced the *súgán* with rush rope (like the ones in our Tea Room today) as after every meal the floor was covered in hay. My mother finally covered the seat of the high chair in oil cloth; I loved shovelling porridge onto the *súgán* to watch it disappear, then I would point to the floor delighted.

By 1945 Lucy's pals were ready to reopen the Peckham Health Centre. Philip went over to London and did more work on the loft over his father's coach house for us. My bedroom was great. He left the main roof trusses exposed so I could have a swing and a rope ladder. My bed was by a window so that when I was in it I could see out over the Butts. This was the local hangout for kids in the daytime and grown-ups in the evenings who walked their dogs and chatted. My mother immediately got half a lorry

Learning supervising skills at an early age. Philip and Paddy Higgins hanging the gate to the White House, designed by Philip and bright yellow.

Down at the strand tasting gourmet sand castle.

Opposite: My eldest daughter Lucy in the family high chair bravely eating carrot soup for a poster to put in shop windows. Lucy thought that she had to keep eating and went through bowls of soup. We thought she was starving.

of sand tipped into the yard beside a tap and I was happy. I loved mixing sand and water to make what I called 'cimint' for building houses and roads. Paddy Higgins, who was in London helping my father with his bookshop, built me a large dolls house and showed me how to put real glass in the windows with putty. He made me paint a couple of wooden boxes for practice before he would let me paint the dolls house. Kathleen MacGillicuddy came over from Kerry to London to mind me as my mother was flat out in The Centre. I will always remember the wonderful quality of Kathleen's voice. She would do anything for me.

Philip had an old brown, second-hand Ford car (made in Cork) with a roof that folded back which he had bought from Lydia Strangman who lived in Kinoith. My memory is that the roads into London were very empty and we would zip into town. Philip had his second-hand bookshop in Harrington Place. He would go to auctions and buy whole libraries and would then arrive at our house and pile books right up to the ceiling of the garage under my bedroom. I was only five, but I soon learned to build houses out of books. Poor Philip would spend all night sorting books then I would come along the next day and mix them all up.

We lived in a great place because canals seemed to come in from all over the country to Brentford docks and from our kitchen window I could see three cranes unloading barges and I'd check whether the barges had engines or were pulled by horses. If there were horses they would be sleeping in a stable down our road not fifty yards from our house and I would take them some apples. At the time I was happy to go around with bare feet. I had long tangled blond hair and I always carried my saw and hammer and a pocket full of nails. I regarded myself as the local repairman. If a board was hanging off a fence, I would nail it back on. If I thought a piece of wood was in the wrong place, I would saw it off. There was a toffee apple shop just down the road and if my mother was ever foolish enough to leave a penny lying around I was off. My favourite part of the day was when the lamp lighter came by on his bicycle. Using a small ladder, he would light the gas lamps on the street one by one. It was magical. At the Brentford Flower and Fruit market I used to wander around smelling the perfumes and imagining what sort of countries things came from. About a mile away, across the river, was Kew Gardens with its incredible variety of trees and flowers, a full size pagoda and very hot greenhouses full of tropical plants. There was a short cut to the Gardens. If I went down a little path by Syon House there was a man with a rowing boat. It cost a penny and you had to wait until there were six people, but I didn't mind waiting, sitting in the boat watching the moorhens, looking forward to the voyage. There was Oster-

Kilmahon House.

ley House, Boston Manor and a little iron bridge over the railway. If a train was coming I would rush up the steps so I could stand on the open planks and allow myself to be enshrouded in smoke and steam. I imagined it made me invisible. If Kathleen was with me she'd kill me because when we got home she would have to wash the soot off all of my clothes and I would fight her as she tried to wash my hair. I only liked having a bath with my father. I loved the smell of sweat from his body. I also remember, in the dim morning light, getting out of bed all sleepy and warm and rushing in to help my mother open and close the buttons on her suspender belt. It seemed magical how stockings could go from silky smooth and shiny to just crumpled. I walked about a mile to school after The Centre closed. There was a little shop with about three things in the window, one of which was a spinning top and I always wanted one as I would see gangs of lads whipping their tops as I walked home from school. I bought one for a penny ha'penny. I couldn't figure it out so I enlisted Paddy's help. Of course Paddy had never used one either. But he was cute, he came from Castlemartyr. "Give it to me and I'll practice and show you tomorrow", he would say. Of course he took it to work and found someone at the local café who showed him. Then he came back to me the real expert.

In London, the thing that changed the course of my early life was the smog. On a damp foggy day in the late 1940s, before central heating, when every house had at least one open fire and Battersea Power Station was in full swing, I would be driving along with my father and I'd put my hand out of the window for a few seconds and it would be jet black. I got hopeless bronchitis and the doctor said to my mother if she wanted me to live she needed to take me back to Ireland as a matter of urgency. I remember my mother used to have a lamp burning strange stuff all night and if I coughed a lot in the night she would come rushing in and sit me up.

Lucy really enjoyed her friends in London and the mental stimulation of her work with them. She was a real ground-breaking human scientist, totally immersed in human health and human possibility. My father wanted to return to Ireland but had no idea how he was going to support his family. I must have been about six then and I was sad to be leaving my first girlfriend, but at the same time I was always mad for new adventure. And so we left London to return to Ireland. I can still vividly remember the airhostess giving me a piece of bright red chewing gum on the plane to Dublin.

Philip travelled to and from Ireland for a while afterwards, continuing to run his bookshop in London. At this time his father was also considering moving to Ireland to farm with Philip's brother, Brian, at Lismore in Co. Waterford. Brian had a herd of Kerry Black cows on a hillside farm with gorse in the top fields, which he would reclaim when he had time. My uncle was one of the founders of the Irish Farmers Association in the 1950s and later went to Ethiopia to advise the son of Haile Selassie on agriculture. After two years without pay, he returned to Dublin to work with Concern. Brian's second wife Eilish McCurtain comes from a line of Irish patriots and her sister Peg, Dr Margaret McCurtain, is a well-known university professor and nun with a global view.

Once settled in Shanagarry, with a lorry load of sea sand in front of the White House and a tap for water, I was happy. Our house was about 200 metres from the sea with a view across Ballycotton Bay to the Lighthouse Island, which winked and honked like an elephant on wild nights. Nothing would grow because of the salt air. Across the untarred road lay my fairyland: Beausang's bog. It was magical. Little tufts of grass poking upwards where a big white hare and rabbits were free to run among the vast array of flowers, blackberries, mushrooms, wild plums and crab apples. I used to wander and dream and really *be* there, immersed in its beauty. One of the most frightening things in my childhood happened one day

Helping Simon get on to our hand operated go-car at The Butts, Brentford. At my right shoulder is Aunt Emily's house. Just above my head is our apartment over Grandfather's Coach House and next door is our Grandfather's house.

when I was playing in the sand – probably making some ultimate imaginary mix of cimint – and my friend Sean and I heard the Murphy's stout lorry coming along the road to deliver to Ardnahinch Bar on the cliff. Sean said, "Let's throw stones at the lorry", so we each grabbed a fist of gravel and I threw it at the cab of the lorry. It stopped and the driver leapt out and chased me. I ran around the house and thought I was finished, literally finished. I can still feel the fear today.

I remember learning a particularly important life lesson one morning when I was six. I got up just after dawn and took my little wooden cart down to the strand for a load of sand. The 'butt' had two bicycle wheels and was beautifully made by the weaver O'Driscoll at Knockadoon. It had all the traditional details in the woodwork and across the front was a pole much like on an Indian ox cart so that two could pull it along. Of course, I put a huge load of sand in and headed up the hill or the 'head' of the road as it was called, from the beach. The hill was steep for a six year old, and less than half way up, I couldn't move anymore. I stood there in my bare feet and homemade shorts. The mist was cold and for the first time in my life I was unable to do what I had set out to do. It nearly killed me to let the cart roll back down the hill and I hated every shovel of sand that I took out. Eventually, I headed home with my small load of sand feeling very miserable indeed. I think that one incident has forged my sense of risk even to this day. I am not afraid of risk, but I am terrified of risk with no way out.

My mother got her hands on an old timber frame, which was about two and a half metres long by nearly two metres high and a little more than a metre wide. She went to a joiner in Cork and got them to keep their scraps for her and I nailed bits all over the frame and made a house. I really loved the bits of tongue and groove which fitted together. Then I painted the inside of the house with pink distemper which I watered down so that there would be enough to finish. I can still remember the clean smell of the distemper, slightly like disinfectant. One day my parents went to Cork. Of course I knew where my father kept his bottles of

At the White House covering the frame with pieces of wood for my first construction. Simon cunningly escaping while he can.

stout. Luckily they were only half-pint bottles as Simon and I finished one off in our own pink house that we had built. Poor Joannie Cusack was minding us and she had to try to explain to Lucy what had happened. Joannie made great apple tarts with a whisked white of egg on top and I would have fun putting in different coloured food dyes.

When I was seven my childhood began to change somewhat when I had to go to school and after moving to Ballymaloe. As a child, Ballymaloe was great fun. Simon and I had a playroom with a trapdoor in the floor where we could use a rope ladder to go down to a hot press. There we would hide and make a raid on Wendy and Natasha Allen, who were close to us in age and living downstairs. Even though we seemed to have very little money to spend, there always seemed to be a whole gang of girls working in the House. At one point there was Hannah White and her sisters Peggy and Mary from Maytown. Simon and I would hide and watch Hannah kissing her boyfriend under the chestnut tree. There was always divilment going on and both Hannah and myself knew no limits. We tormented Mr Bauer, an old German refugee whom the Allens had taken in and who could make anything out of nothing. He played the zither and made amazing Christmas presents for all us kids. We also stole Tom Crowley the gardener's motorbike, burnt Bob the Painter's hat and reared dozens of mice which my cat ate all of in one night. Some people called me a holy terror. I like to think that I was just active and hungry to try out new things.

I loved the old and new farm buildings with

A 'crissie pressie' for my mother maybe 1962. Photo Lauren Pearce.

the smell of fresh beet pulp, the smell of pigs, silage and grain steaming in the drier. I used to drive a little Ferguson tractor very slowly while the men loaded bales. Dan Dolan and his wife Mary used to invite us to their house for the evening (they had no children).

Ballymaloe had a jersey herd and the milk and cream were to die for. I learned to lay concrete blocks building the dairy from Mr. Bauer who butchered the boy calves for veal. Myrtle then made Weiner Schnitzels, small thin pieces of veal dipped in egg and breadcrumbs. As kids we loved Schnitzels.

When I was young many foods were semi-sacred. We ate strawberries twice a year at their peak. Salmon might be eaten twice in the summer, poached and served with homemade mayonnaise and cucumber that had been thinly sliced and salted the night before. Lucy said that this procedure made the cucumber more digestible. Vegetables were eaten in season. Probably the reason my mother was such a good cook was because she applied her intelligence to having very little money most of the time and so she had to watch the cost of her raw materials very carefully. This of course is what started the great French food tradition: learning to use cheap bits and pieces. Luckily right up to the 1960s Ireland was totally organic. The chemical companies hadn't fig-

Lucy caught just waking up in her favourite chair at Kilmahon.

ured out how to piggyback onto the food industry. Therefore any carrot or spud or meat that she bought was almost sure to be natural. In a speech Lucy gave to a food conference in England in the 1940s she famously said that in her opinion one of the greatest social changes taking place in Britain was the changing focus of farmers from growing for nutrition to growing for profit. I remember as a child in Shanagarry that there was a real pride among small farmers in the quality of their milk, eggs, or new spuds and also a tremendous generosity of spirit. What then happened to farming felt very like what is happening to the whole country post Celtic Tiger. I have to have faith in the human spirit and hope we will learn and move forward.

With no fridge or phone or car I find it incredible how my mother developed her cooking skills. There were periods in the 1950s when we just could not afford meat. Michael Cuddigan, our excellent butcher from Cloyne, when asked why his beef was so tender would reply, "I only kill the female of the species." Michael also fed grain and meal to his animals for the last number of weeks before slaughtering them. He used to deliver meat to us twice a week, and when we could not afford it he would continue to deliver bones for the dog. He always left enough meat on the bones for my mother to make a couple of burgers. Lucy knew well that this was his way of helping her without appearing to give her charity.

When Myrtle Allen decided to open a restaurant Lucy was very excited at being asked to help and advise and she went into overdrive. Because now the challenge was to produce good quality home cooking with a unique touch that made economic sense. There were piles of books constantly on our dining table, mainly Elizabeth David, a long time friend of my mother's. There was a book by Constance Spry and Rosemary Hume, the English women who had a Cordon Bleu cookery school in London and who were famous for always peeling grapes in their salad. There was Mrs Beeton and Julia Child and Larousse Gastronomique. All of the experimenting at Ballymaloe was done in Myrtle's home kitchen whilst dealing with us very liberated kids. I can remember one day running past my mother yelling, "I hope all this doesn't mean we won't get a nice dinner." Poor Lucy.

We next moved, when I was twelve, to Kilmahon, a rectory dating from 1780, which was very different. There was none of the farm activity or building of Ballymaloe; Ivan was always building. I really got the meaning of peaceful beauty there. My father had finally found his vocation in making pottery. There was a calmness in our lives. Lucy was in her element cooking in the large, stone flagged kitchen and had a wonderful vegetable garden. I remember one evening many, many years later, just before we finished work in the Pottery I was carrying some clay across the yard and my mother at the age of more than seventy was running full tilt across the cobbles with an armful of freshly picked vegetables. I asked her what was going on and said she should be careful not to break her neck on the cobbles. To which she replied that she had just been reading one of her favourite cooks who advised when you pick your vegetables to run to the pot before they lose their freshness. She thought that was a great idea. Mary Gowing, a very influential copywriter whose main account was Coty, was my first of three godmothers. She gave us six Albertine roses which my mother planted at different points around the house so that in the spring there was a heavenly perfume. Kilmahon was a very easy, friendly house, and I adored my father's respectful, modern ideas in the old setting. In the school holidays, I always seemed to be building. After Mr Bauer at Ballymaloe, Danny Power, Ritchie Higgins and Moss Aherne were great teachers.

My mother had big plans for the garden but unfortunately for her there was never enough money

to fully fulfil her aspirations. Occasionally in the spring, she would buy half a dozen very small shrubs. I used to cut the grass and was forever mowing down her young shrubs: something that confuses me looking back now. I think it's very male, choosing not to notice something. I have always regarded myself as more sensitive and female than male, maybe it's the artist in me. I use my intuition a lot, logic is not my mantra and I try very hard to be open and in touch with my feelings. I have never really got 'being a male', but remembering my life as I write it, I see bits of latent male showing from time to time. It doesn't feel like me but I also know that it is a real part of me. Like my competitive side and the being prepared to fight to the death in some situations. Also not noticing what I choose to not notice, almost as though some things don't exist. Ask most women and they will grin knowingly at these traits.

I really was a misfit at school. In fact, I have always been a misfit in society. It seems that my sense of reality is different to almost everyone I know, except my father and my son Oran. It's like we live in a different place. To us it seems obvious the way we are, our value system and our relationship with integrity. Maybe other people are like us but don't express it. I don't know. One of the extraordinary things that I am just discovering is that I never really know anyone. I have a sense of who you are but then come the surprises. It's amazing to me that marriage as an institution has lasted this far. I wonder will it go on? I am not declaiming love but for me love and marriage are not necessarily compatible. I say this as somebody whose first marriage didn't work, but whose second marriage is one of the greatest joys of my life.

For me, life stopped when I went to school. It was like joining the army. My person vanished and I was trying to play catch up to a foreign way of being. It was against everything I had been up to this point. I was crossed off the list of items on the planet by a large pencil in someone else's hand. School was like death. This wondrous bubbly piece of infinite possibility was unplugged and put away far out of my reach. Look around you. Very few people have the energy or focus to survive this savage act of being sent to school. If people were willing to rerun their memory of the first month of school I'm sure they would be shocked. The big winners would be those who had had their creativity knocked out of them before going to school. I suppose it's not surprising that the people running the world mostly haven't a clue due to never having been allowed to develop their true intelligence. What they have developed is a hard shell and an appetite for control. When you live in fear, control seems like the cure.

From the age of seven to eighteen I felt kind of dead inside, and then until I was twenty-five I always seemed to be clawing my way back from the trauma of school. That's not to say a lot of amazing things didn't happen in those years. I just felt shackled by chains, unable to be me. I remember that while I was at boarding school my mother home schooled two of Ivan and Myrtle's children. I was very jealous; and so I retreated into the only areas I felt comfortable, gardening and woodwork.

At Saint John the Baptist Protestant National School in Midleton we had a wonderful teacher called Pearly Lynch. I know she really loved me and whenever she saw I was totally lost in boredom she would suggest I go out and do some gardening. I would bring in flowers from my garden at Ballymaloe and Pearly would bring me primulas from her garden. She taught all six classes together in a small Victorian room with a modest coal fire. We made lumpy cocoa at break time and Shirley Tait, a lifelong friend, used to do my sums for me. Because we had no religion at home, I had no idea that it was a Protestant school. I used to love going to the birthday parties that the Taits, Kingstons and Jeffries all had. John Jeffries and I used to curse like troopers.

My parents had a dear Quaker friend called Arnold Marsh who had a very open attitude to education, rather like A. S. Neill in England. As a result, at the age of nine I was sent to Drogheda Grammar School where Arnold was headmaster. His sitting room was rather like our own and I felt very comfortable with him and his wife Hilda. She was a painter and she taught me how to make rush mats and all sorts of other crafts. I hated being away from home though. After a couple of weeks I was helping Arnold do some gardening. The school was practically broke at this stage and Arnold taught lots of subjects and even subsidised the school himself. One day, while gardening, Arnold said to me, "Stephen, you don't seem to enjoy class do you?" I said I didn't. He then said, "I'll do a deal with you. I'll buy you three little pigs, and they are totally your responsibility. You can feed them on school waste. You clean out their house. You don't go to class at all but you have meals with everyone else and you must keep busy doing things you enjoy doing."

I painted lines on the tennis court. I mowed the lawn. I made a wardrobe for my mother. I went up the four-storey roof taking nails and slates to the roofer fixing leaks. I built myself a little house out of bricks after we knocked down a wall. I got on my bike and went up the Boyne and cut reeds to clad the roof of my little house which was about two metres long and a metre wide and propped up against another wall for support. I used to charge seniors a penny to smoke in there in the winter. I wouldn't let them take their girlfriends up to my straw bales in the pig yard though in case they smoked and started a fire. Arnold had once been a lumberjack in Canada and during a heavy snowfall he helped me to build an igloo. It was about two metres in diameter and about a metre and a half high. The trick was that we made a wooden mould and packed the snow in to make solid blocks. The cold spell lasted a while so I opened a bet on when the last drop of the igloo would melt. In the end, I needed a bit of protection as some pupils argued about when the last bit of the igloo actually melted.

I was ten then but very independent. After the pigs were fattened and sold, Arnold asked me should he buy me some more. I said no I thought I'd like to try going to class. Because it was my choice I caught up with my four months absence in a matter of weeks. We were living at Ballymaloe when I went to Drogheda and I stayed there just under two years. One Friday, Arnold came into our pre-school assembly and said that the school was broke and that he was going to a Dublin Quaker Meeting to ask them to take over the school. On Monday, he reported that he had got a good response and was hopeful but, as it was no small undertaking, he would have to wait for confirmation. Arnold must have been over eighty at this time.

Because both Arnold and I were impossible to classify, people often thought we were mad and Arnold didn't get the credit he deserved. Right up to the end of his life Arnold never looked at anything with the accepted view. Like me he always said, "What if?" I'm sure he very much reinforced this tendency that my parents had encouraged in me. If school had such a negative impact on me, Arnold had the complete opposite effect. He was an altogether inspiring character.

It was at about this time that Philip started making pots with Willie Greene in the greenhouse at Ballymaloe. I made my first pot there in 1953 when I was ten. When I moved from Drogheda to Newtown School in Waterford I was twelve and our family had by then moved from Ballymaloe to Kilmahon in Shanagarry. I started in second class but the dreadful Billy Boggs moved me straight down to first class for not knowing what 0.75 was. I was very jealous of Simon being at home while Kilmahon was being done up.

If school had such a negative impact on me, yet Arnold was such an inspiring character, how do I square that away? Simple, I wanted to be at home with my mother. I used to cry a lot at school and wet the bed but I learned to survive. I don't believe it's natural to be sent away to school so young. Years later when I was on the committee of Newtown, there was a very small boy running around the school and everyone minded him a bit. I think his parents may have been killed in a car accident and so school was his home. I felt like I was that kid and I never dared go near him in case it broke my heart. Thirty or more years before I went to Newtown, Arnold had been there and had saved it from bankruptcy. Arnold's way of running a school was on total trust and so everything was pretty open-ended. Having been at Drogheda with Arnold I could see how the rules that he had made at Newtown had lost their point due to a lack of trust. Consequently, it was hard to do woodwork as every tool was locked away and one needed permissions that were hard to get.

Luckily, the headmaster Liam Glynn was a family friend and an inspired human being. On one of my first days at Newtown, three senior boys from sixth class took me to their changing room and told me I had to clean their rugby boots. I asked how much I would be paid, they said, "Nothing". So I said, "No". They filled a wash hand basin with water and were about to stick my head into it. I caught the nearest one to me and smashed his head into the basin so hard that I broke the basin and blood poured from his head. The two helpers ran and I went to report to the headmaster what had happened, figuring that Liam was a decent honest man and he would agree that I was entitled to defend myself against bullying. I never heard another word about the incident except that one of the bullies who was doing a line with my cousin, complained that I was very rough. I then started cleaning boots at sixpence a pair. I was really good at it and worked out a production line so that they had a brilliant shine. It became one of my projects at school as a way of standing up to the bullies. By the time I left six years later I think we had succeeded as all of the boys in my year agreed with my view on bullying.

About a month after I arrived at Newtown I was called to see Liam. The staff had been bellyaching to him that I refused to call the men 'Sir'. I have always had the idea that there are not greater or lesser people, just people, and so I try not to look up or down on anyone. When Liam questioned why I refused to call the masters Sir my reasoning was clear, "Where I come from it is not usual for the employer to call his

employees Sir." Liam got it and being the fair-minded man that he was said, "Stephen, could you try to do me a favour, the masters are on my case about this and it would be a great help to me if you would try calling them Sir for a week, then come back and tell me how you feel about it." So, to help him out, I did and later agreed for the sake of peace to continue.

Sweet little rock'n'roller, super self-conscious.

Having figured out how to actually learn at Drogheda, schoolwork was no problem. I participated strongly in class, did minimal homework and no revision and trusted my memory. Unfortunately we had an alcoholic sadist as a maths teacher who never taught me a thing, which is a pity as I have a great capacity for numbers. It wasn't until I was sixty-two that I stopped having nightmares about Billy Boggs. Fortunately for me, Newtown had a small farm run by 'Fef' as he was called, father of the historian Roy Foster. Fef was from the midlands of Ireland and understood country ways. For some reason he liked me and saved my life many times at staff meetings. I think – although he couldn't be seen to agree – he really got what I was about and gave me as much space to be myself as he could. Isn't it great when someone really gets what you're about? He gave me a little garden so that I could grow carrots to sell and I in turn cleaned out the pigs and cut the grass.

By the age of twelve school was just an inconvenience that I endured in between working at the Pottery during the school holidays. At fourteen I was forced to play rugby and hated it. I much preferred making stage sets for the school play. Then I picked up a guitar. For me, it was all about the performance. At sixteen I started doing Elvis impersonations at the school dances. Surprisingly, I also became rugby captain having moved myself from second row to number eight so that I could have more fun. I had some truly wonderful girlfriends at school. It was all very innocent, but equally very exciting.

I remember one night at around ten o'clock being woken by Wendy Allen in our house in Shanagarry. Ivan and Myrtle were outside in the car waiting to take us both dancing at the Showboat in Youghal. The Johnny Quigley Band from Derry were playing. It was before the whole showband thing had really kicked off and there were only the Quigley brothers and the Clipper Carltons leading the way. This was the beginning of my interest in music. The array of musicians on stage playing a variety of instruments amazed me. At times there would be two trumpets, a trombone and two or three saxes. Jackie Flavelle on bass, and an incredibly shy guitar player, very like Artie McGlynn, who soon appeared with the Platters from Omagh. It seems like everyone in the North who didn't have a gun had a guitar and they just kept coming. The Freshmen, Them, Rob Strong, Earl Jordan... I never knew music could be so good.

I walked through the intercert (the Intermediate Certificate) in 1960. I really enjoyed it and did fourteen subjects. My favourites were agricultural science and woodwork. I am told that I came top of woodwork in Ireland with ninety-six percent. The next year I completely lost interest in school and fell in love with several girls. I totally adored these girls. They were my whole life. It was just kissing and spending time together. I really got what female energy was all about and the girls seemed to enjoy what I was about too. I certainly wasn't your average lad destined to become a bank manager (but thankfully I have known some really great bank managers who helped make many of my ideas happen).

I literally nearly went mad during my last year at school. I tried but found it impossible to concentrate in class. School work held nothing for me. If what I am doing doesn't interest me, I can't do it. I suppose I have a bit of a donkey in me. There came the point early in sixth year when I was codding myself that I was working but I was somewhere else entirely. I reached the point when I didn't know who I really was, nor what I wanted, nor where I was headed. I had no sense of my own reality.

For about six years after I left school I was pretty much out of control. I followed various notions I had, but nothing made me happy or gave me pleasure. I have always had an amazing work ethic and discipline

Gerard Pringle's drawing of Philip's Pottery.

and so I drove myself forward, but only because I was driven to do something, even though I didn't know what that something was.

I remember walking away on my last day of school in 1962 and realising that most of the people in my class had spent the last two years aiming for careers. I had been totally focused on girls and hadn't given a career any thought. I had a sense that I would enjoy being a forester or a carpenter. I had been planting trees in a field of my father's since I was ten and I loved watching them sprout every spring. One of the first things I did every school holiday was to go and check on my forest. I still like to visit and talk to my trees. By good fortune I planted them in the field where I later built my house. Leaving school, I decided that before choosing a career I would give two years to helping my father sort out his Pottery as a thank you for him having given me so much.

My life has always been a series of contradictions with no clear direction until a direction arrives. (This applies particularly to travel plans.) I have an aversion to planning my future in case it limits my possibilities. I hate insurance, as it is as unlikely to pay out as religion. I hate the idea of pensions. There was an eight-year-old boy in the Pottery one week and my son's dog, Sensi, was racing round like a lunatic. The boy said, "Are you not afraid that the dog will break things?" I said, "No, it's a bit like when you ride your bike. Are you afraid you'll fall off?" I have always tried to avoid being fearful of what the future may bring me. Consequently, I am mostly pleasantly surprised.

I never chose to be a potter, and I have only recently realised that pottery chose me and it has been and always will be a very exciting journey. Becoming a potter was more a matter of strategy than passion. My number one choice would have always been to be a rock singer. I really know how to engage and hold an audience. Just after I left school some pals who had a band asked me to sing a few songs with them at a dance. The girls all started to scream and drove me on. I knew I could do it. When women scream at you like that something basic and extraordinary happens. A natural two-way recognition takes place and it builds. I will never forget that feeling of power, being wanted and wanting to give more back. However, I was not really a musician; I found timing difficult, I hated rehearsals, I was afraid I would forget bits that we had agreed and as I had a rough singing style I constantly suffered from sore throats. I like my health and the idea of constantly travelling and eating rubbish at odd hours (when I already had a stomach ulcer) meant that I had to decide these were memories to be cherished, but not the path for me. **S♣P**

Sharpening a chisel to continue building pottery shelves.

Opposite
Top: Philip packing for post
Bottom left: Nora's bike outside the front door of our house.
Bottom right: Pots waiting to be bisque fired at Philip's circa 1960. Traditional Youghal jug upside down.

This page and opposite: First pottery shots on Shanagarry Strand, circa 1958. Photos Alan MacWeeney.

PHILIP
BECOMES
A POTTER

"Dreaming is sacred."
Stephen Pearce.

Philip on old Leach foot wheel. Behind are three old traditional Youghal pitchers. Below is Willie's money box better seen on page 18.

W hen Ivan Allen wanted to buy Ballymaloe in the late 1940s, Philip borrowed money from his father to help with the project. After having spent all of his own money doing up his half of Ballymaloe House, and not enjoying farming at all, Philip went through an intense period of prayer and meditation, aided and abetted by Phineas Bury, the then Dean of Cloyne.

One morning he woke up having had a very vivid dream and told my mother. She said to him, "I know what you've dreamt," because she had had exactly the same dream. She told him to get into the Land Rover and go to the pub in Youghal where he would meet Willie Greene. After that Willie came to live with us at Ballymaloe. My father bought a funny old wooden potter's wheel which was designed by an English potter, Bernard Leach (a potter yes, but an engineer no). Willie showed Philip the clay field and all of the old Youghal pottery shapes. Philip was smart enough to realise that slavishly copying the traditional shapes was not the way to go, and besides, he had his own vision. My father was in his forties at this stage, and generally to be a skilled potter you need to start potting in your early teens. Undeterred, after a year of fiddling around in the greenhouse at Ballymaloe where he set himself up, Philip cut a deal with Ivan Allen whereby Ivan exchanged Kilmahon House in Shanagarry for part of Philip's investment in Ballymaloe.

Philip was very interested in glaze and form and so he went to Cornwall for a year to study with Harry Davis at Crowan. Harry was brilliant at glaze technology. Wanting to share this new experience, in 1952 my father organised for Willie, my brother Simon and myself to take the Inisfallen ferry from Cork to Fishguard and then on by train. Simon and I were left at our grandparents' house in Cardiff to watch the Coronation on the telly as my grandmother thought it was very important. I remember Simon and I flew a large Irish flag from Grandad's high flagpole. On the train journey, which was by steam engine, we sat in a little compartment with sliding glass doors so we could see everyone passing in the passageway outside. Willie would head off to the bar every once in a while and come back with another pint bottle. If we kicked up enough we would get a bottle of lemonade, although it wasn't as good as Irish red lemonade. Apparently, when Willie arrived in London he decided that he didn't like the English so he took the next train home with the money my father had given him to go on to Cornwall.

After a year my father came home. Willie didn't stay on much longer. He had advanced TB, endemic in Ireland at the time. No one was certain of a cure and my mother was nervous having him in the house with small children. I think by this time the drink had a fierce grip on him and I always suspected that may have had something to do with him leaving. Certainly his pots had become very wobbly and feeble. But he was a great old rogue, loved by everyone and the last in a long line of Greene potters from Youghal. It must have been strange for Willie, having been part of a family that had worked very hard and achieved a high standard of production and proficiency, to come to us in his old age, well beyond his glory, and maybe feeling that my father was a clueless amateur who would never fully understand. Thank goodness we found him though. It is through Willie and all of his blackguarding that I feel connected to a long line of real potters.

Shanagarry Pottery started in the greenhouse in Ballymaloe. It wasn't called Shanagarry Pottery then, my father just felt inspired to make things. I doubt that the possibility of selling what he made ever crossed his mind. Maybe it did though, as my mother and her friends were making, ahead of their time, children's clothes in our sitting room. I quickly learned to make baby's bibs from different coloured towelling with an initial sewn on the front. It wasn't a huge leap for me; after all I had been knitting scarves for my dolls and teddy bears for years. It is highly likely that Philip thought that he too could sell a few pieces of pottery having seen Lucy selling her wares to Brown Thomas in Dublin (voted the most beautiful department store in Europe in the 1950s).

Having learnt about glaze from Harry Davis in Cornwall and the basics of pottery from Willie, my father was ready to give pottery a proper try. So he did his deal with Ivan and we moved to Shanagarry in 1953. At first, apart from the clay preparation shed, the Pottery was just one small downstairs room off the main house. I don't think my father had the courage to start in the barn in the courtyard in case it didn't work. He was of the age when the wisdom was to wonder, "What if it doesn't work out?" After a couple of years the Pottery did move across the yard to the barn and the original workshop became the showroom. It stayed that way from 1955 until my father's death in 1993. Even though he started the Pottery when he was forty-two, he still got more than forty years out of it, proving that it's never too late to start something new.

It seemed that anyone who visited our showroom was invited to lunch. My poor mother. At one o'clock my father would arrive into the kitchen with four complete strangers and by two o'clock we would all be the best of pals. It's amazing how many of those strangers were really interesting and became long-term friends. One day Ove Arup (then the world's leading structural engineer) was brought into lunch. I'd never heard of him and I told him that I thought that structural engineers were a waste of space and that when I built I just knew intuitively what to do. I invited him out to see a shed I was building. He said he

thought that my main structural beam was a bit light. I told him that it would be grand. He was staying at Ballymaloe and did the calculations and got his London office to re-run his numbers. Next morning he came over to apologise and tell me that I had used exactly the right sized piece of timber. I totally admired him for that.

Another time, Émile Noël, who was head of the European Economic Community in 1958 (now the European Union), and his wife Lise called in and soon became close family friends; they had two daughters, which was always a good thing. Lucy had prepared lobsters for supper as the French were fanatical about shellfish. When Émile saw a whole huge lobster on his plate he said, "Please, nobody speak to me for forty-five minutes. This is a religious experience." Years later when Émile was president of the European University Institute in Florence (from 1987 until 1993, before our own Paddy Masterson), I would spend weekends with Lise at their Paris apartment in Monge on the Left Bank. In the early morning we would go out and choose fowl and fish for the weekend and suitable veggies. There would be poking of chickens and the sniffing of fish and shaking of vegetables so that we weren't paying for water. Lise was much loved by the traders as she really knew her stuff. We would go back to the apartment for breakfast and then hit the cheese shops and patisseries. The cheese was to die for. My experience is that the French, if you can generalise, don't usually spend a lot on wine but they really know value for money and which wines to drink with various foods.

Thinking about the early years now it is incredible how innocent and amateurish it was. Our horizon was very close. We had no ambition or vision. We just went to work and made pots. The driving force was that they had to be pots that we liked. Preparing clay, digging the garden, chopping logs, life was all very manageable and real – as with the farmers I visited nearby who were just doing what needed to be done. Interestingly, although Simon and I have climbed some great heights in our lives, we both have this very simple bottom line of liking to light a fire, cook, receive a meal and feel at home. I have a sense that that is what almost everyone wants deep down. For Simon and I it's a case of "You can take the man from the mountain, but you cannot take the mountain from the man." Another thing that runs strongly through our family is our trust of people and what life brings us. Many, many surprises come along both comfortable and uncomfortable, at least that's the way I interpret events.

Having decided to move from Ballymaloe to Shanagarry my father did up Kilmahon House in a very interesting way. Built in 1780, it had been a rectory to both Protestants and Catholics with a wing added in the 1860s during the Famine to generate employment. Philip respected its fine Georgian roots but gave it a very subtle 1950s style with lots of cutting edge Danish furniture. I have been fortunate that both my parents had impeccable design taste and also lucky that my godfather, Patrick Scott, was always on hand with his amazing simple ideas. His paintings are my favourite objects on this planet. Pat introduced Philip to Gerald Pringle who came to pot in Shanagarry. Gerald was also a huge influence on me and made some wonderful pots. Having been an actor and producer at the Gate in Dublin, Gerald encouraged me to sing and write songs and generally encouraged self-expression. He was the type of older person you could talk to about a lot of things you couldn't talk to your parents about. Gerald lived in a little old farmhouse with a huge fireplace that must have cooked for many a harvest threshing. The house had once belonged to the Batt brothers and hence was always called 'Batts' which was one of the reasons why Gerald liked it. (I like that in those days possessions were often known by the owner's family name. For example, 'Bulla Pearce' was my brother's dog.) He had a very delicate feel for life and managed to impart that to the pottery. He used to work on the glazes and it was he who came up with the ancient Celtic imagery that sometimes adorned the pots.

Interior of our family kitchen in Kilmahon, way ahead of its time in the 1960's.

Having spent just over £1,000 doing up Kilmahon and buying second-hand pottery equipment, my father had two objectives: firstly, to make pottery that he felt comfortable with and secondly to pay the school bills. The Pottery mantra was simple: useful, affordable pottery for everyday use. And so it has stayed.

Gerald was happy playing around with a few pots but Philip, having converted the outhouses to process his clay (at the time he was the only potter doing so apart from Carley's Bridge, an old traditional Pottery in Enniscorthy), now needed to get production going, so along came Paddy Fitzpatrick. Paddy was eleven years old and was getting a hard time at school because, like me, he was not a bookish person. One thing that hasn't changed is that people with manual ability like Paddy Fitz and myself are still regarded as second-class citizens at school. If you are not academically minded you are a loser at school, unless of course you are good at sport. When will we ever learn? At two o'clock in the morning is a professional person going to come and fix your plumbing? Anyway, Paddy kind of morphed into the family, helping here and there in a very disorganised way. Lucy insisted that Paddy have lunch at the Pottery and so he always had the same food as us but with loads more spuds. Paddy was a great man for the spuds. His father, Dan, worked for the village forge and we used to call in to watch the white hot metal being shaped into gates and horse shoes and little bits of ingenious things used to fix farm carts and implements. It was a time when you fixed everything and threw nothing away. When I made shelves for my father I had to pull nails out of boxes and straighten them to use again. My mother used to collect the twine from parcels into a ball: a treasure from which I often used to steal bits for my own projects. A farmer I knew in West Cork used to go to Skibbereen on his donkey and butt (as carts were then called) to do the shopping on a Saturday. Coming home he read the local paper while the donkey knew the road. When they arrived home he would fold the paper neatly and leave it on the gate pier with a stone on top to stop it from blowing away. Another man, who would be peeping out of his window in anticipation, would come and collect the paper. This was repeated three times until it returned to the owner. Then the paper would be used to wrap school sandwiches all week. The children would carefully bring their pieces of paper home each day until finally it would be used to wrap eggs.

There was a pond in our front field by the road where Jack and Dave Meany, two old bachelor brothers, used to dig clay for fixing their hearths. (In those days in Ireland when people used to cook on the open fire, often on a Friday they would fix the sides of the hearth with clay and white wash it for Sunday.) By way of return, if I was passing the road and Dave was up on his rickety old ladder putting a patch on the thatch, I would be allowed to take the scallops up the ladder to him (scallops were made of willow split lengthways down the centre and then used to secure a bunch of thatch to the roof). Dave was very cranky and to be allowed to help him was a great privilege. He had never heard the old Irish phrase *'Ní hé lá na gaoithe lá na scolb'* ('The windy day is not the day for thatching') and often the sheaves of rushes would blow away and I would be clinging to the ladder terrified that I might drop the scallops and receive the height of abuse. I loved it though; it was such great gas. Thank heavens I was brought up before health and safety regulations were invented.

At fourteen my parents decided that it was time for Paddy to start on the potter's wheel. The thinking at that time was that as Paddy's father was a blacksmith then Paddy should also be good with his hands. I have no idea what Paddy thought of all of this, maybe he just did it without thinking at all. The result though is that when Darina Allen wants dinner plates today she insists on Paddy making them. My brother in America, fifty-seven years later, insists that Fitzy make his coffee jug.

With modest production came modest sales. My father took me to Dungarvan to the weekly market and I would sit on a box beside a man selling cypress trees. I had a few mugs and jugs and a platter or two. I sat all day and sold one mug for a shilling (the equivalent of about fifty cent today). The day was regarded as a great success: at least one person in Ireland liked our pottery. We were on the road!

In 1954 my father organised a display of pottery for Christmas in a hardware store in Cork called Scotts. Everyone was very kind to us even though I'm sure they thought we were mad. I mean, why would you buy one of Paddy's heavy lumpy mugs when you could buy bone china with roses and gold rims to put in the glass cabinet? There we were anyway between the sledgehammers and paints. My father had a real knack for display and the pottery looked amazing. Then along came Dr J.B. Kearney who spent almost £10. We were made. A known art collector and a man of distinction liked our pottery, or felt sorry for us. Whichever it was, he got some great pottery at a great price. I could hardly lift the box out to his car.

Almost fifty years later when J.B.'s granddaughter Dairin was getting married J.B. gave her the key to the cellar where he stored his surplus Shanagarry pottery. She had twenty minutes to choose as much as she wanted. I subsequently became close friends with Dairin's husband Cathal Deavey (but that is for later in the book).

Emboldened by our Cork success, Philip set his sights on Dublin. I really don't know what we would have done in our lives without Pat Scott. Pat introduced my parents to Senator Ned Maguire who owned Brown Thomas. Ned's son John was full of ideas ahead of his time as well as being very much into modern design. In 1962 we put a few pieces of our pottery on the glass shelves next to Waterford Glass in the basement of Brown Thomas. As a moment in history it was a bit absurd: these funny lumpy jugs next to Ireland's pride and joy. Out of a Christmas order of twenty-four beer tankards, thirteen were returned unsold. Undaunted, John Maguire said that we should have an exhibition in his gallery, The Little Theatre. He chose a fortnight in July because the Horse Show would be on in the RDS and a lot of the smart international set would be shopping at Brown Thomas. My moth-

Paddy Fitzpatrick just getting the knack.

er then had the brainwave that, as we were totally unknown, we should have someone well-known to open the exhibition. At that time there was a great cook called Monica Sheridan on Ireland's new Telefís Éireann and the women of Ireland, including my mother, were in love with her. Her great trick was to lick her fingers on the show from time to time, something that was considered rather risqué at the time. Lucy thought that people would come to our exhibition to see Monica in person and then my mother would also have the opportunity to start what would become an on-going friendship with her.

My father and I set up the exhibition and my mother came up by train with bunches of roses freshly cut from our garden that morning. I was eighteen and I remember being self-conscious and every bit a teenager that year. I wore a dark brown leather vest and a cross on a gold chain, my hair was below my shoulders and I was emotionally in chaos. What I really wanted was to be a rock star.

The exhibition went really well. We sold about £160 worth of pottery over the two weeks. This was at a time when the working wage in Ireland was just under £10 a week. Of course J.B. came to support us as well as a good few Dublin trendsetters. I can no longer recall their names but I do remember thinking, "Wow, if this person likes my father's pottery it must be ok". Our whole family loved our pottery; we would have died for it. I still would. But however much we believed in the pottery, it was a very personal statement. My father wasn't commercial and he was always true to himself and the pottery.

In those days Grattan Freyer was the first renowned 20th century Irish craft potter. Then came Peter and later Helena Brennan working in stoneware. The least likely person to succeed was my father and other potters took him as a bit of a joke because of his simple, innocent pots. One by one the other potters went their way, leaving Shanagarry Pottery to carry not only the flag for Irish craft pottery but the whole vision and ethos of craft in Ireland between 1952 and 1965. There was a small number of excellent crafts people both young and old, but none chose to drive it to become a known name like we did. I will always be grateful to Muriel Gahan for her early encouragement and support. I will also always be sorry that when she asked me to take on the Country Shop from her when she finally retired that I didn't, believing at the time it wasn't my thing. At the same time Blanaid Reddin was a rock of strength to us through her various incarnations with Bord Fáilte and Slieve Bán Cooperative in Strokestown, Co. Roscommon. Then there was Rosalie Fitzgibbon of the Irish Shop in New York who also supported us.

There was a very remarkable man running the Irish Export Board, Córas Tráchtála Teoranta

(CTT), called Bill Walsh. He was smart enough to put Paul Hogan in charge of design, a man of vision who in 1961 dreamt up and organised a group of four Scandinavian designers to visit the barren landscape of Irish design. Paul had a passion for design and a strong sense of marketing and we soon became close friends. More than anybody else Paul was responsible for the Kilkenny Design Workshops project in 1963 that Bill initially asked my father to head up. One day, Paul arrived at my parent's house with two of the Scandinavians. One was the top designer Kaj Franck from the Finnish company Arabia – the trailblazer of modern ceramic design – who later invited me to go and work with him. I will always regret that I didn't, as apart from being a great designer, he was a great human being. He was modest while obviously being absolutely brilliant and, while I thought there would be delicious food in his house, I also knew it would be lovely to simply be around him. Paul unloaded from his old banger of a car a picnic feast of fresh lobsters and a nice sharp Loire wine. My mother made mayonnaise and served her fresh brown bread and we spent several very happy hours together discussing life and design. Apart from Pat Scott and my parents it was the first time that I had met serious designers and I felt an urge to travel beyond east Cork. Halfway through the meal my mother noticed that Paul was not there and sent me to find him. He was under his car covered in oil fixing the gearbox. He explained that by using his car he got paid mileage and he needed the money for a down payment on his dream house in Sandymount in Dublin.

After their tour the Scandinavians held a seminar at the RDS in Dublin, which I went to rather unwillingly with my mother. To my surprise, there on the table in front of the Scandinavians were two of Paddy Fitz's early wobbly jugs. A furniture designer from Denmark called Erik Sorensen was talking about design and Ireland and remarking that design hadn't really been in the national psyche and that if Irish household products were to be sold outside of Ireland then some serious work needed to be done. Either Paddy McGrath, owner of Waterford Glass, or his chief designer stood up and said to Sorensen, "If you know so much about design and are so critical of us, what should we be doing differently?" Sorensen smiled and said, "How much will you pay me?" and then sat down; the point being that no value was placed on designers or design in Ireland at that time and Waterford would have been the main craft export. Towards the end of the seminar the Scandinavians held up Paddy's wobbly jug and said, "This is what design is all about." A year later, in a book published after the seminar, only three Irish products were deemed fit for export without any design improvement: Shanagarry Pottery, a tweed from Donegal and Muriel Gahan's Irish Homespun Society's hand-knitted jumpers. Paul Hogan's answer to the design seminar was the Kilkenny Design Workshops which were to be a hotbed for Irish design and which brought lots of talented international and Irish designers together. Unfortunately, design is not something that can be state run as it needs a commercial edge. It was great fun however and certainly not the worst use of money in the history of the state.

This recognition by internationally acclaimed designers and the subsequent reports in *The Irish Times* and *The Cork Examiner* put Shanagarry Pottery in a new place. We moved from being considered a joke to being taken seriously. We had been no competition for the bone china tea services with its roses and gold rims. The few people who had bought our pottery had also put it in the glass cabinet suspecting that it might be special but not knowing how to use it. People referred to Shanagarry pottery as "that heavy black and white stuff", or "the nun's pottery" because of the black and white glaze which with its furry collar.

Eventually people began to drink their tea from our mugs and once they started they couldn't stop. Surprisingly to us, people felt really comfortable using our cups and wanted to share this discovery with their friends. When a neighbour would call in they would be offered tea in a Shanagarry cup. If a positive comment was forthcoming the host felt endorsed and knew what to give as a present. Our mugs are our ambassadors and in 2013 we still sell the same mugs that Paddy still makes.

I recall a time when Paul Hogan asked us to make a bowl for the Irish ambassador in Washington to present to John F. Kennedy on St. Patrick's Day. Gerald Pringle made a series of beautiful, wide, open bowls so that the Shamrock could be laid out in them. Unfortunately Waterford had the political clout. I heard afterwards that the wisdom was not to send something from an unknown when Waterford was selling millions in the States.

In the summer of 1962 I was finished with the torture and torment of school. It's not the teachers' fault that doers like me are totally bored and frustrated by a system that has no direction, makes no allowance for individuals and which tries to homogenise us into what can become a boring, dry society with young men

committing suicide by the dozen. I tried very hard to fail the Leaving Certificate because I knew my mother would want me to go to university. When I passed, my mother, being the observant woman she was, had already realised that I was destined to do things with my hands. I had been working flat out in the Pottery every school holiday for five years, which in its own way had been a great relief from going to school, but I was very good at carpentry and loved planting and minding trees. My father's pottery was not doing well however and, as I was not ready to leave home, I decided to work with my father hoping that between us we could make a success of the pottery, and that's what I did. I was remarking to Myrtle Allen of Ballymaloe recently how happy I was that my father had made such a success of our pottery. She replied, "Go away out of that – it was you who drove it forward!"

I remember the first pot I made in 1953 when I was ten. I can still smell the clay and the ripe grapes that hung over the rickety foot operated potter's wheel in the greenhouse where my father learnt his craft from Willie Greene. It was at about five in the evening and I was watching my father struggle with the slippery clay when he said to me, "Why don't you have a go." I felt shy and frightened and tried to duck the offer but, as I was sure that I could do better, I sat on the wheel and yes I made a better pot than my father made. However, try as I might, it was another six years before I managed to do it again. Seeing how difficult it was to control the clay and knowing that my father was stony-broke, I became obsessed with helping him make the

Above: Lucy at home scooping cream onto crab. Photo Pedro Guerrero circa 1958 for House & Garden.

Opposite: Philip in his study.

pottery viable. When we moved from the grape house at Ballymaloe to Shanagarry I used to prepare clay, fix roofs, cut down trees, build storage racks, paint, plumb and much more. I was fanatical about making the Pottery happen.

My father, like myself and indeed my children, was a hippy and a free thinker. We all like to row our own boat. Often when I tell Oran and Mirin, my son and younger daughter, about the freedom and fun of the 1960s and they realise how controlled the world is that they are heading into they say, "Do you think we could find an island somewhere with no government and no stifling rules?" I know the feeling, because that's exactly how I felt when I was their age, and still do.

So at eighteen, as I was walking away from school, I made my snap decision to help my father for two years to try and put a shape on the Pottery. In one sense he had already done it. He had a very clear design philosophy: simplicity. He understood how to relate to his customers. Everything was useful. The business was like a plane ticking over on the stand. It just needed driving down the runway full tilt. This somehow scared the hell out of him. I suppose even though he was a very remarkable man in many ways, like most of us he was the one person who didn't see anything special about what he was doing. **S♣P**

PART 2
MY JOURNEY

ADVENTURES & DISCOVERY

Laying blocks for clay shed. I can't figure how my hair was so short as I was about 20.

"Life is what happens while you're busy making other plans."
  John Lennon circa 1963

After six months of preparing clay, packing pots and building shelves and a clay store with my father I realised that Shanagarry village was too small for me. I needed a broader experience of life and other Potteries in order to take my father's Pottery forward. I greatly admired the work of English potter Michael Cardew, whose bowls and mugs I had used as a child. My father, who as a young man had gone everywhere on his bicycle, used to buy Cardew's pots as seconds off the Pottery wall in Winchcombe, Gloucestershire for thrupence each in the 1930s, and perhaps it was this early introduction to Cardew's pottery that made me want to go and work for him in 1963. I went to England on my Honda 50. There was a propeller plane from Cork to Bristol which took five cars, a motorbike and passengers. It cost me a mere £5. When I got to Winchcombe I had a timing problem with the engine of the bike and so Sid Tustin, the foreman of Michael Cardew's former Pottery (which was now in fact owned by Ray Finch and known as 'Winchcombe Pottery'), sent me to his pal who he promised me was "a world expert so ee is." When I found the mechanic he was in his late seventies, stone-blind and worked from his garden shed. The first thing he said was, "She sound pritty strange, she do. We'll av a cup a tea then I'll av a look at er." Of course the cup of tea was so that the engine could cool down and he could feel his way round with his fingers. I called back the next day and my dear Honda was lying in bits on the floor. There were no two bits of the motor still attached together. He guessed at my fright and said, "Never seen one a'these before and couldn't resist taking a good look. These Japanese are pritty cunning. I don't see ow an alloy head can take 20,000 rpm. I'll av'er back together tomorry evenin' as right as rain." The next day, there she was purring like a kitten. He wouldn't let me pay as he said, "That were an education that were; made my year, never even dreamt a'those mechanical possibilities."

Sadly for me, Michael Cardew was in Africa starting a Pottery in Abuja in northern Nigeria. Luckily however, Ray Finch had made the Pottery very much his own and instead of Michael's lively earthenware Ray was working with stoneware, which was new to the UK at the time. Ray was like a father to me. He lovingly

Sid Tustin taught me to throw pots.

taught me all that I was prepared to learn. Bear in mind I had hair down below my shoulders and was very independent. At the time the Beatles were just starting; in fact I went to the first night of the tour that made them famous. It cost seven shillings and sixpence and I was hoarse for a week from screaming. The mothers of Britain were locking up their daughters because of the disgusting long-haired boys. Well we've all seen the photos, but even Mick Jagger's hair when he arrived paled into insignificance beside mine. One day in Patrick Street in Cork when I was passing Woolworths I overheard one *shawley* say to another, "He's like a vision of our Lord." I smiled and walked on as I knew in her innocence she was thinking of that picture of Jesus that hung in every kitchen. I took it as a huge compliment.

With Ray Finch's guidance and knowledge I learnt about production and glaze; and how to pack pottery for the post. I had packed pottery before for my father, but this was a whole new ball game to me. We would spread out bales of straw, wet it with a watering can and then trample it before packing. I believe the theory was that damp straw would cause less dust when unpacked. On top of that the water certainly made the straw much more pliable and a better packing material. After a morning packing in a dark smoky loft with the sunlight from the two skylights showing just quite how much dust was in the air, Sid came and asked had I packed the pots as instructed. I said yes, but actually I had packed them according to my father's system as I knew we never had any breakages. How was I to be sure that these English potters knew what they were on about? After all the English made my father's Mini Minor which was always breaking down and when PJ O'Heas in Cork ordered a part from England it took forever to arrive. Sid kicked three of my parcels down the stairs and told me to unpack them. Not a thing was broken. "So" Sid said, "now that I've shown you, always do it like that." I never told him the truth and went on packing like my Daddy did. Sid brought me to Cheltenham railway station one Saturday afternoon to see parcels being loaded onto the train. It seemed like the guys were just trying to break the stuff the way they were handling the boxes. Sid said with a smile, and in his deep Gloucester accent, "That's why we never use them fragile labels. Like a red rag to a bull them are." And he was right.

As the junior apprentice I would be sent out to the cider orchard to wash the clay in preparation for using it. I had an unreliable pump for drawing water from the stream and a couple of old rakes that turned in a slow horizontal circle and washed the stones and nettles out of the clay. The liquid clay then went into pits in the ground which were lined with soft bricks. If I scraped the bricks with my shovel when digging the clay out Sid would kill me as his pots would be full of stones. The clay I was preparing was earthenware clay. As a mark of respect to the Winchcombe tradition, and because Sid refused to make stoneware, ("them stoneware wallers" he'd snort in disgust), Ray allowed him to continue to produce a limited amount of earthenware. As I was under Sid's supervision I too got the occasional go at making beakers. This was a real sign of Sid's fondness for me as you don't normally get to make pots early on in an apprenticeship. I was lucky. I made mugs and mugs

A selection of early pots from when I was looking for direction in the mid-seventies. Top; My mother's idea for a lamb stew pot. Tall and narrow so that she could easily scoop the fat off the top before serving.

and more mugs, thousands of them. I made them so well that when I returned to Shanagarry I made mugs and mugs until one day my father needed some bowls, which were far easier to make, and so I began to make a mixture of pieces.

Sid had one amazing trick. When we production potters (as opposed to makers of one-off individual pots) make the first pot of a batch, we generally set a pointer according to its exact size and then use that as a guide so that the whole batch turns out the same. Sid used a porcupine quill stuck on the front of the wheel with a piece of clay as his pointer. Now, as his wheel was beside a large window where the sun poured in, there is no doubt in my mind that over an eight hour day the pointer would rise up about a centimetre as the clay holding the quill dried out. Yet all of Sid's mugs were the same size. I used to ask him his secret and he'd just say, "Someday you'll find out lad." He would never tell me. Well, last year, more than fifty years later, I figured it out. I was on the wheel playing with some shapes using the same amount of clay to make cereal bowls as I did when I last made them thirty years ago. I measured the bowl and to my surprise it was spot on the right measurement. The thought went through my head, "Sid, you cunning old fox, you knew the size of the pot in your head but set the pointer out of habit, and so you'd look like you knew what you're doing." It was a bluff. *Sin a bhfuil.*

During my apprenticeship Michael Cardew sent a constant stream of Nigerian students to us for the 'English experience'. I really enjoyed the Nigerians. They had great names such as Danjuma Ladam, Peter Bute Kuna Gboko and Gugong Bong. The guys did nothing. Work was not on their agenda and, whatever way you went about it, it was a disaster. Ray thought I might be able to handle it and so I was put in charge of student activities. They were lovely people and when I worked out that it was easier to do their work for them and just talk to them, it was great. Something Ireland and Nigeria had in common at that time was that both the Kilkenny Design Workshops and the Nigerian Department for Trade saw pottery as the way forward. Maybe it had something to do with the fact that it didn't cost much to set up a small Pottery. (Actually for my money, Kilkenny Design should have focused on wool and taken advantage of all the skill we had in the country at the time.) Meanwhile, in Nigeria Michael was spending so much time dealing with the Civil Service there and his bad health (the two were most probably linked) that he did very little of what he did best – making pots – and so the Pottery in Abuja struggled on in the blazing heat with lots of cat-napping and possibly some very nice weed being smoked.

While working at Winchcombe I had visited the Craftsmen Potters Shop, off Carnaby Street in London, with Ray Finch. It was his main outlet and had a large selection of different potters' work on display. Going around the shop I immediately liked Richard Batterham's pots as well as those of

the renowned Australian potter Gwyn Hanssen Piggott. After finishing at Winchcombe I got onto my trusty Honda 50 and headed south over the Cotswolds to visit Richard and Dinah Batterham. They then pointed me to Gwyn who was working at Wenford Bridge, (Michael Cardew's new Pottery). I went from Gwyn's to the Bernard Leach Pottery at St. Ives where I bought Bernard's old electric potter's wheel, and then right on down to the tip of Cornwall to Scott Marshall whose uncle made all of Bernard's pots at St. Ives. As I returned I stopped off at four more Potteries on my way to Bristol airport. Some time later I returned to work with Gwyn in Cornwall and also with Mick Casson in Buckinghamshire.

A few years later, my father and Simon and I went to visit Gwyn in the centre of France at the potters' village of La Borne near Bourge. There, historically, they had both the oak forests to fire their kilns with and a unique deposit of clay similar to that of Bizen in Japan. Gwyn had bought an old, falling down house in a hamlet of three or four farms. There was quite a community of potters nearby but Gwyn preferred to be on her own. The house was a complete wreck but with incredible ancient charm. It had huge oak beams, a topsy-turvy old slate roof and old farm tools everywhere. Even the old hay was still stored upstairs and we constantly found old usable saucepans to put in the huge kitchen fire in the smoke stained main room. The gable end had just fallen out of the house and so Simon and I set to digging foundations and laying French blocks (large clay bricks with holes running through them). On the second day Gwyn hired a French mason to be sure we were doing it right. It was very hot and so the mason had a gallon milk can of what we thought was wine to drink as he went along. Not to be outdone we put up our own gallon of wine and by mid-afternoon we were ossified. Simon and I figured that no Frenchman could drink that much wine and so we watched next morning as he filled his can with water and put half a cup of wine in. Farmers out haymaking by hand in Ireland in those days would have a milk can of water in the shade to which they would add a sup of separated milk. Both systems make the water slightly tart and so cut your thirst. The best cup of coffee I ever had was in France with Gwyn. I would go over to the nearby farm for a can of fresh milk and Gwyn would make the coffee. Incredible. While staying with Gwyn (who was not actually making pottery in France at that time) on different occasions over the next couple of years, I chose to help out other potters I admired in La Borne and absorb the atmosphere of their workshops.

One evening, after Simon and Philip had gone back to Ireland, Gwyn, myself and a Canadian poet called Gerry, headed into Sancerre for a few drinks. When we returned to Gwyn's mini van with its GB plates there was a group of local thugs waiting to beat the shit out of *les anglais*. In those days, all French workers wore a cap called a *casquette*

Above: Gwyn Hanssen Piggott at La Borne with breakfast. Below: The poet Gerry doing what he did best...

(a peaked denim cap that John Lennon also used to wear). Gerry and I sensing the danger started swapping caps and talking pidgin French. After a while the French guys went off in disgust as they could see that they weren't going to manage to get into a fight with these jokers. Gerry and I just lay on the ground in hysterics while Gwyn played Purple Haze on the car's cassette player. She always did have good taste in music.

The summer of 1964 was a big one for me. I left Winchcombe and came home to help with what had become an institution: The Brown Thomas Exhibition. I had a few of my first tentative pots in it. Apart from a few terrible modern shapes I was already beginning to head for plain clay with white glaze. I also made a few all white pots with black rims, which I must make a few more of some day as they were pretty cool.

The beauty of the Brown Thomas Exhibition was that my father and mother could display the full range of our pottery in a way that people could see how it would build into sets and also how they might use it. My mother's displays of flowers in our vases and bowls piled with fruit were wonderful. Even today retailers don't do this. Luckily in Ireland people know the pottery now, but then, when the idea of choosing each item to go on your table was unheard of, it was really important to reach out and show what was possible with our pottery.

As soon as I returned home from England, I started to think of ways to escape again. However, I also began to see what my father was doing with his life. His pottery had a very pure, simple design philosophy behind it. He was not just making pottery, he was responding to a very direct and true calling of the human soul to express what *is*. If you take a plate or a mug of my father's it does not say, "I'm special, look how clever Philip Pearce is". It doesn't scream, "This is where fashion is". Rather, it reflects the purity of form and function married together. His plate was and is a plate. It holds food. Its simplicity allows the food to speak and when the plate sits there empty it just is quietly there. My father, along with my brother and I, all have this total design integrity. Whatever we do or whatever we make, there is a oneness. Sometimes it comes easily, at other times there are months and years of trying to let go of 'clever' ideas so that the simplest solution has space to show its face. I have been very fortunate in having my parents, my godfather Pat Scott and the English potters Lucie Rie and Richard Batterham to look up to. Pat paints pared down, simple white and gold symbols on natural linen. Lucie Rie was an Austrian potter who worked in London and made natural porcelain pieces with pure lines for daily use and Richard makes great stoneware, which to me expresses English and Chinese traditions in a true and sophisticated way. None of them ever compromise on what is so, and it is different for each of us. That is the wonderful thing. We just have to have the courage to trust in ourselves and the timeless process which we are all a perfect part of.

Above: Fantastical stew pot.
Previous page: Kevin spent hours chopping bits off apples so they would look casual until there were practically no full apples in the bowl!

In the world of design a lot of energy seems to go into being clever and unique or different. All of these things happen naturally if you let go of trying. Try, and one usually comes up with something common or ordinary and with a very limited shelf life. When I have a strong impulse to make a mug, for example, I sit at my potter's wheel with about twelve ounces of clay (which I know will make a good size mug to hold) and make my idea. Then I change it a little and after about six tries I give up and let it make itself. Two years ago I decided to design some new shapes and spent three months making nothing but mugs, hundreds of them. I wasn't happy. Then one day, without thinking, I mixed up the measurements for the height with those of the width and it was perfect. Is it luck when that happens? Or perhaps do we get tired sometimes of swimming against the tide we've created and just surrender to it?

Both my father's Shanagarry pottery range and my own range are timeless classics: simple in the extreme and minimal. There are traditions in handmade pottery. We don't follow any. Travel the world and our pottery always stands out as unique. It is not because we planned it that way. It is be-

cause, when we made a new piece, the design ethos was always to do away with complications and unnecessary nonsense. As a teenager I often made special pots for my mother: casseroles, stew pots, coffee pots. Looking back now I see they were often horribly complicated. Lucy would cook a stew in the oven and say how much she liked the pot. A few days later, in an off-hand way, she would say something like, "When I was washing the casserole the rim and handles were hard to wash and I wondered how it might be if they were slightly simpler." I soon learnt that she was always right.

During the summer of 1964, while working in Shanagarry, I started talking to Bill Walsh at Córas Tráchtála about going to Mexico because I liked their innocent use of terracotta and their old ceramic figures were magical to me. From my time in England having seen so much stoneware pottery, I now knew that I wanted to continue with my father's earthenware tradition. I had become very protective of what we made against the scorn of the British. Stoneware had become so fashionable in England and all the non-pottery countries (by this I mean places without great pottery histories unlike China, Korea and Mexico for example) that the earthenware of Shanagarry Pottery was considered a second-class citizen. In my opinion, stoneware is a soft option. The chemistry of glazes and fitting them to your clay is much simpler in stoneware. Furthermore, unless you are very lucky, stoneware clay looks like concrete and I love the soft gentleness of earthenware and porcelain.

When I went to see Bill about my grant to travel for further training, he told me that Mexico wasn't possible but that a group of town planners from Dublin Corpo had just been to Tokyo to study city planning and so Japan was on the radar for getting a grant. Ireland was like that then: a young island finding the rest of the world. My line to him was, "You are trying to grow exports and you know that you need good designers. I'm the hottest thing you've got, but I need to get out there and see what the opposition is up to". He agreed and offered me £300. I said no, I wanted £1,000. After a nice lunch together we agreed on £600. I went down to Paul Hogan's office to complain at how tight-fisted CTT were and he suggested trying UNESCO. Following his suggestion, I wrote to D'Arcy Hayman, the then head of Arts and Cultural Planning in UN-ESCO in Paris. She told me, off the record, that in terms of education Ireland was a third world country and that I would be entitled to £1,000 to further my specialised education. It was around this time that Philip and I were at our annual Brown Thomas exhibition when in walked a Japanese couple, Mr and Mrs Imaeda. Kuni Imaeda was Professor of Cosmic Physics at the Dublin Institute on Burlington Road. (How weird is that when we hardly had a tarred road from Cork to Dublin?) They liked our pottery and recommended that I should go to study in Japan. Mrs Imaeda added that her grandfather was a close friend of the top potter in Japan. I said, "Yes please!" And so it happened. I left Paul Hogan the job of collecting my grant money from UNESCO and forwarding it on to me in Japan so that I could leave immediately on my trip. And this, my friends, was how the CTT Kilkenny Design Scholarships were born. Two years later, I was asked to put together a committee to continue the process and I said no, just to give the grant to my brother Simon, which they did and he went to study glass all over Europe before setting up his workshop in Bennettsbridge, Co. Kilkenny. In turn, the following year Simon was asked to choose two people. I suggested to him to give it to Ken Thompson and Nick Mosse. He said, "I can't, they're friends" and I replied, "Ok, so think of two more promising people". And so Nick went to Japan and Ken to Italy. In terms of bang for their buck, it was one of the best deals our government ever got. I hope the scheme still exists.

I decided to travel from London to Tokyo on the Trans-Siberian Express in 1966. It only cost £80 then, including the boat trip from Vladivostok to Yokohama, eighteen days train ride, a hotel in Moscow for three days and a hotel on Lake Baikal for another two days, plus all meals, which included a lot of caviar and vodka. I read *Anna Karenina* on the train. When finally I arrived in Tokyo I was met by a niece of the Imaeda's. The next day she brought me to a small private gallery to see an exhibition of Korean and Japanese pots that were between two to three thousand years old. The trip to Japan was worthwhile for that exhibition alone; it changed my life forever. Emotionally still in full revolt, thinking I was the planet's number one hot shot designer and here in front of me were all of the precious, unique ideas I had in my head, and more and better. Unfortunately, at that time I had not read Steve Jobs' famous quote, "Good designers copy, great designers steal." Ironically, Jobs was paraphrasing Picasso who may have been paraphrasing T.S. Eliot and so on. I have a real sense that ideas are out there just floating around and that like a television set we can draw ideas from the cosmos if we just relax and do it rather than fuss about how clever and unique we are.

Japan was unique and very different from anything I expected. Pat Scott taught me his only word of Japanese before I left, *hisera*, an ashtray! I had been to England, America and France, but Japan in the mid-1960s was extraordinary. It fed my soul in so far as there was a tremendous expression of, and respect for, the very ancient, side by side with the ultra modern. I wandered around Tokyo in a dreamy daze. In the 1960s the Japanese still seemed to be hanging their heads from World War II. Sony seemed an odd name to call a company and the Japanese were nervous because one of their first products, a rice steamer, had not worked. Then Mr Honda, always the innovator, decided that he wanted to make motor cycles, which were a huge success. He made his first sports car with a chain drive against the advice of everyone in his company. "We make moto-bike!" was the cry. I tried to talk Honda into giving me one of their new cars to drive back to Ireland with my brother. They only cost the equivalent now of €400 but I think they were nervous that it would break down and we would have no way of fixing it. Later Mr Ibuka, the founder of Sony, invented the Walkman which prompted a deputation to Mr Morita, head of sales, begging him not to produce this stupid gadget. Morita's reply was "Ibuka designs, you make and I sell. Thank you." It became their most successful product. Honda cars haven't done badly either.

I took the new, ultra high-speed bullet train, down to Bizen in Okayama Prefecture where the most highly esteemed objects are made for the Tea Ceremony, a much revered and ancient tradition in Japan. The master I was to work with, Tōyō Kaneshige, was the most famous of hundreds of potters in the area and indeed within Japan. *Numero uno*. In fact he was a 'Living National Treasure', an honour bestowed on him by the Emperor himself in 1956. It was by pure chance that I went to Bizen, where the kilns have been firing since medieval times, but it was the perfect place for me. No glaze. The pots pick up colour according to where they are placed in the kiln. The clay itself is very unusual. It looks like stoneware but is classified as porcelain. Climbing kilns were used which were fired with pine for about a week. In places where there is not much movement of air, ash builds up on pots and forms a glaze. In other parts of the kiln flames rush past leaving different colours. When carefully fired by top potters pieces come out looking like they are weathered rocks on a mountainside with patches of moss. Because Bizenware looks like a work of nature it is the most prized pottery for the Japanese Tea Ceremony: flower vases in many shapes, bowls for drinking tea, little jars for tea powder with individually-made lacquer tops, water bowls and plates for cake. There were also a few pieces that had nothing to do with tea, such as sake bottles and sake cups that came in every shape imaginable. Tea Ceremony is a kind of cultural religious experience where one is very present and aware of everything: the process, the forms, the flavours, the history. It is one of those Japanese

Preparing clay in Japan, 1966.

cultural art forms that is totally scripted and controlled and when the master gets it down pat, after years of study, he should arrive at a place where he is totally free and the ceremony should appear fresh and alive.

Tōyō Kaneshige made the most extraordinary pots. Like my father's and my own pottery, they just *are*. He had the knack. He was in his early eighties and only made pots in the spring and for one month in the autumn. He used the best clay in the area, which was expensive and dug from under rice fields after which the field would then be replaced back on top. (It makes sense to have rice fields on top of clay so that you don't waste water through soakage when flooding the fields.) I used to have to break twenty centimetre blocks of hard dry clay with a hammer and then pick out even the smallest stones by hand before crushing the clay to dust in a large pestle and mortar. Then I would mix the dust with water and leave it to dry for several days in clay dishes before making a pile of about 300 kilos on the mud floor in the workshop. The clay now had to be worked by foot for many hours and then stored in blocks in a cool cellar for a few months. The Japanese were delighted to have me do this work for them despite the fact that they hated the smell of our sweat.

One thing I learnt in Japan was patience. On one level it was an amazing experience: this old potter doing everything the old-fashioned way. He even had a girl from the hills turning his wheel by hand with an over-sized chopstick. The house was ancient with a thatched roof and the food was old-fashioned, simple country fare. I slept in a loft in the shed over the workshop. My room was about two by two metres and one metre high. I would climb a ladder and then crawl to my bed. Most evenings we would have a bath in a cast iron cauldron like Irish farmers used to have for boiling food for pigs. The grandmother, *obasan*, would be outside the window stoking the fire under the pot on top of which floated a round piece of wood about sixteen inches in diameter. Before getting into the tub you would wash yourself using a cold hosepipe and some hot water scooped from the bath. Getting onto the round wooden board and sinking it to the bottom of the cauldron without falling off and burning my feet was quite a trick. I knew that the granny was probably stoking the fire extra for me and would report to the family what she thought had been going on from the noises I made.

The bit that nobody had told me was that, when requested by the local Cultural Centre to take on a foreign student, a Living National Treasure could not say no. So, when the student arrives the plan is to make his life unbearable so that he will quickly leave. The host still gets credit for inviting a guest while the visitor is regarded as ungrateful for leaving. This was usually how it went - until I arrived. Being Irish, laid back and wild, I was not into all the Japanese culture and etiquette in the same way the American students were. Americans would arrive and bow to the guy and know his work, know about Zen, Ikebana (the Japanese art of flower arranging) and Tea Ceremony. They would speak Japanese and be very serious; I knew nothing. I had wanted to go to Mexico and had ended up in Japan, which had been a way of getting out of Shanagarry. It was quite a few months therefore before I realised the Japanese torture that they were inflicting on me, firstly by putting a 6' 2" Irish rugby player into a 3' 3" high bedroom. In the mornings, I would get up at six thirty and sweep the mud floors with a small hand brush and then prepare the clay. When I was called in to breakfast it was made very clear that the mountain girl had reported that I had done everything wrong. The next morning I didn't get up until the call for breakfast only to be told that I should have stayed in Ireland if I was going to stay in bed all day. The next day I got up early and just waited for instruction, which never came. The question at breakfast was why get up if you are going to do nothing. The following day I got up and tried to get things right, but to no avail. And so it went on for four months when Kaneshige moved me out into a little old hotel which he paid for because, as I now know, he would have lost face if he threw me out. By then I had heard stories of an American female student running to the train station in floods of tears after just two days. I think that before me the record was that of a Californian on a Fulbright scholarship who lasted five days. Without knowing it, I had become a kind of local legend. When I went down the street, which was lined with Potteries, potters would invite me in to drink tea or a beer and try and find out what sort of person could outgun Kaneshige. One day I was up running in the hills when a pick-up truck pulled up alongside me and a potter called Michan beckoned me to get in. His father had been given a hill for services in colonial wars and the three sons had built a shed there where their mother and their wives cooked. The boys and their father made pots and drank. They took me in and it was like night and day compared to where I had been. They had an old aunt called Yoshida *obasan* who rented me a large room with a balcony and I built a little kitchen downstairs out of packing cases. It was then that I released Kaneshige from his obligation. He said that I was much better suited to the Sakakibara family as they had no culture. I told him that I really liked his pots but as a human being he stank and that I was happy to have finally found some good decent Japanese people. In those days, the agricultural wage in Ireland was about £10 a week and Kaneshige got between £10,000 and £20,000 for a tea bowl the size of a cereal bowl. Kaneshige would make forty bowls in one morning. He worked three months of the year.

I really had some great fun with the Sakakibaras. We did everything in the Pottery shed. It was a single-storey shed with a clay floor, a stove in the middle of the room and a tin roof that was supported mainly by rough-hewn wooden poles cut from the mountain. One side had four pottery wheels facing out through a series of sliding windows. The granny was always there cooking for us and for the grandchildren. The three wives were also there as well as *ojiisan*, the grandfather, whose hearing aid kept falling out. It was a bit like an old Irish farmhouse with everything going on at the same time. The men couldn't wait till six in the evening when we would start drinking sake and then supper would come in bits and pieces. They were the kindest and most generous people you could possibly imagine.

On the 24th of December I was telling them about Christmas in Ireland and how we eat turkey. Immediately, we all got into the back of the pickup truck and down to the local battery chicken farm with balaclavas and bags to steal six chickens. Back up the mountain and into buckets of hot water to loosen the feathers and the plucking began. All of the meat was taken off the bone while one brother roared back up the hill and returned with sixty half-gallon bottles of sake and a load of beer. The chicken was served raw as *terri sushi* with soya sauce and wasabi. The meat was still trembling it was so fresh but the sake took care of that. We also had dried squid and pickles. The party went on for three days with the granny constantly coming up with new dishes. On New Year's Eve we had a big problem. We were in a karaoke bar singing our hearts out when in came one of the Sakakibaras' old school buddies. He was building a local technical college and had to have the roof poured by midnight; it was then nine thirty. So into the back of the pickup and down to the site we went. It was a three-storey building with a flat roof and there were nineteen ready-mix trucks queued up waiting to unload. There were three concrete pumps, unfortunately all at one corner of the building. Light was poor, supervision nil and dozens of wheelbarrows were strewn everywhere. I suggested we take the concrete to the furthest corner first. I was told no, just dump it wherever was nearest. If you think that the Japanese are organised you should have been there. Apparently the concrete had to be poured by midnight so as not to incur a huge technical penalty. The fact that some poor divil would then spend hours sorting out the levels wasn't a consideration. I hope someone put a good layer of asphalt on that roof! Eventually we went back to the Pottery for a nightcap and then lit the kiln, which traditionally brings good luck if fired on New Year's Eve. We prepared the salt and sake peace offerings to the kiln god and lit the kiln. The first stage of firing a big multi-chamber kiln is very slow and eventually we fell asleep. Early in the morning the women came and woke us and we relit the kiln. By late afternoon the kiln was going fairly well but we fell asleep again so the women put some booze in a shed and locked us in and took over as it would be unthinkably unlucky for the kiln to go out three times at such an auspicious time of the year. A day later we were let out and told to go and have a shower and come back to finish off the kiln which is hard work as the fires are really consuming timber at this stage. The other reason we were let out was because Kyoto, the middle brother, was the expert at understanding the final stages of firing. It was bitterly cold on the mountain with ice and heavy snow. I had got myself an old cardboard box that a tumble dryer had come in and set it up beside the hole where I was throwing in sticks as a shield from the wind. This was before we fell asleep for the third time. As I slept a lighting stick fell out and set my jeans on fire and I was woken by Michan throwing a bucket of water over my legs. Thanks Michan, these legs have walked a lot of miles since.

One fine evening the brothers insisted we go fishing. I had been telling them about Shanagarry being on the sea and how I like fish. We went across a long bridge to their mate's fishing boat. It was about a 15-foot punt with an outboard motor. We took a couple of large bottles of sake to be drunk cold and a bucket of fresh water. We had a small little trawling net which must have dragged along the bottom of the water. Every ten minutes or so we would haul in our net which would have glass bottles, music cassettes, condoms, mud and seaweed. In among the crap we managed to find a few nice large shrimp. We washed them in salt water and then in fresh water, took off the heads and ate them raw, sashimi style, washed down with sake. After a good session of this we went back to the port. There were several large sheds with fish tanks in them containing a great selection of different fish, alive and waiting for a buyer. The guy who had been driving the boat got a net and scooped out a fish with a big balloon in the front of its throat. We lit a fire and through his drunken eyes, he prepared the fish. In the middle of the feast someone explained to me that this *fugu,* or puffer fish, is the most dangerous to eat because if the person preparing the fish isn't an expert the poison can leak from its skin or organs and the person who then eats it can die within minutes. All of the way back to the Pottery I had my head out of the truck vomiting. I asked Michan did he think I needed to see a doctor about poisoning. He replied cheerfully that what I needed was a good shot of sake because if I had eaten any poison I would have been dead long ago.

I made almost no pottery in Japan. I was a young, production-minded twenty-two year old. My whole mindset was making simple things to use. The potters of Bizen were in a place of pure history and were unconsciously drawing on the roots of creation. At twenty-two I couldn't even begin to go there. They were in the same mindset as the guys who built Newgrange. I felt that I was witnessing something very special but at the same time they pissed me off with their arrogant preciousness. And so I decided to go into absorb mode. No matter how foreign or strange anything seemed I just absorbed it: food, culture, pottery... the works. I didn't express myself through making pots. I just watched, touched, smelled and trusted that if what I was experiencing had any relevance to me it would express itself when it was ready. And it has done so often and in unusual, subconscious ways. Japan deepened my appreciation for craftsmanship of all kinds, from baking a loaf of soda bread to making ugly Victorian jewellery.

At the same time I was very lonely in Japan and it took a mammoth effort to survive emotionally. But I am stubborn. I lost about thirty-five pounds in weight but I taught myself Japanese by watching soaps on TV and by learning pairs of opposites such as high/low, big/small, wet/dry. Screw the grammar. I have developed this system for any new language I need to learn and it works pretty well. With hello/goodbye, please/ thanks and a whole head full of opposites I can communicate most things in many languages.

To earn a few bob, I taught English at the local cultural centre. There were three other English classes taught by Americans with textbooks and grammar. All students were beginners. I just did conversation-based teaching inspired by my own experience as a foreigner travelling around Japan with almost no Japanese. I would pair the students up and give them a situation, for example like when trying to buy a bus ticket from our local town to Tokyo. The American teachers thought my students were a bunch of no-hopers until the end of the year when each class put on a show. The Americans' groups went up on the stage terrified, giggling behind their hands. I had told my girls that if they giggled I would kiss them. They knew by then I was a man of my word and it would be unthinkably embarrassing. The Americans' classes recited complicated poems and made stilted speeches. I then lined my gang up behind the stage in pairs ready to do short everyday scenarios totally spontaneously. If they got tongue-tied the next pair would come on and say, "Thank you very much everybody, clap please" and then begin their scenarios. We brought the house down. I had insisted that we go on last. The Americans thought it was because I was afraid that my gang were inferior but I knew that we were an impossible act to follow. What had seemed spontaneous had been rehearsed with dictionaries in coffee shops and at home and on school buses but it came out fresh and vital. There was one girl whom I really fancied and we would go for a walk after class and watch the moon rise over the Castle. In the six months I was there I was never allowed to kiss her or hold her hand.

My brother Simon had been working in a Pottery in New Zealand with Harry Davis, the same potter who had taught my father glazes in England back in 1953. We met up in Tokyo soon after Christmas 1966. I was so happy to see him. I showed him some different pottery regions there and then brought him to the hot springs after which we were going to hitchhike back to Ireland.

Life in Japan is really a ballet. As crowded countries, I always sense that England and Japan face the same challenges in terms of the logistics of running the country. The difference is that the Japanese have it handled, both because the infrastructure is in place and the population understands that for things to work they must forfeit part of their freedom and privacy so there is a social code for everything. By the time Simon arrived in Tokyo I had become part of the system. To see him full of vitality, with his big heavy boots and huge rucksack, full of life and coming off a boat full of Australians who had been drinking and partying non-stop for days, was quite a culture shock. During rush hour, Tokyo subway trains had professional pushers with white gloves who would line up with their backs to the wall and charge to push everyone on the train so that the doors could close and the train could stay on schedule. Simon and I would stand just inside the doors and at every stop when the pushers charged we would roar like lions and take a step forward. The poor pushers would stop in terror and amazement. After about three stops everyone in our carriage would clap after each performance.

In the countryside, toilets were a hole in the floor with a giant pottery tub way underneath. The crap was scooped out twice a year and put on straw mats on the pavement to dry a bit before being spread on the rice fields. In summer when you used the toilet the mosquitoes would fly up and bite you on the ass. There were many rules and niceties about toilet use. One was that the shoes you changed into before entering were made of rice straw or plastic and were always coloured green and kept outside the toilet door. You would change from the normal house slippers to loo slippers and back again, and then when going to a *tatami* (rice mat) floor you went barefoot. Simon wasn't used to this, especially after a few drinks and several times I saw him coming onto the *tatami* mat in green slippers. This posed two problems. Firstly, manners forbid the host from saying anything. The second problem was the sense of pity for the poor unfortunate who arrived at the toilet door to find no green slippers. He couldn't go in because to enter in his bare feet and then go back on the *tatami* was unthinkable. To go back to the *tatami* and ask Simon for the slippers was impossible, as it would be pointing out a shortcoming in a guest. Worse was to come. One evening Simon came back from the loo with a grin from ear to ear and whispered in my ear that he had dropped one green slipper down the loo, so now there was only one green slipper outside the door. As everyone was looking at me expectantly I explained the situation apologetically and respectfully. I then suggested that we should all practice hopping on one foot in anticipation of going to the loo so as to deflect attention away from Simon's misdemeanour or literal faux pas. We did and were all hopping around the room like eejits until one of the wives arrived at the door smiling with a new pair of green slippers.

One of my greatest pleasures in Japan was going to the *onsen*, the natural hot springs. This is another Japanese religion. Groups of people, maybe up to 200, go and stay at a spa inn for a few days to eat and do karaoke but mostly to sit in the mineral waters, often out in the open landscape. In Japan the public bathhouse and the *onsen* are the social leveller. Men talk and make friends in a way that in everyday life is impossible due to social structure. There was no preoccupation with nudity and older women sit in the rock pools and caves (at the Matsue *onsen*) in fine weather and snow, chatting to friends and strangers alike. Beside every *onsen* is a noodle bar, usually a battered old hut where you sit up to a rickety plank bar and are served by an old granny. The fare is simple, mostly cold udon noodles in a clear broth with ice and finely chopped scallions, plus of course beer and sake.

I was fortunate enough to meet an American who had married the daughter of a top sushi chef and who had his own place in Beppu on the South Island. Beppu is one of the most prized fishing ports in Japan and the selection of fish there is extraordinary. Before this sushi to me was not particularly special but by the time I left Beppu my opinion of sushi had completely changed.

Another thing that fascinated me about Japan was the geisha. In Beppu I stayed in a room right beside where they trained. The geisha tradition is one of very high culture; they sing, play music, dance and accompany men to social occasions (sex is often not on the menu). Their clothes and the arduous training are very expensive. Their aim is to have a patron who finances them and occasionally they become very rich. The patron in turn is someone who wants to own a woman so incredibly beautiful, well-mannered and attentive that he gains more prestige in the eyes of other men. This contradiction in Japan really fascinated me. There is this very high cultural tone and also a very base vulgar side. I remember helping a top potter to fire his kiln; because of his status his pots would have been in the realm of cultural icons. At one point during the firing a helper pinned a Playboy centrefold on a door and the potter and his lads started throwing darts at the poor girl. Coming from Ireland it felt very strange watching, as I was in awe of the pots inside the kiln.

The main reason for Simon meeting me in Japan was so that we could hitchhike back to Ireland together. The journey took three months and cost us the equivalent of €40 each. We had nothing like a plan and neither of us was too hot on geography. Mostly it was a question of finding a petrol station, buying an Esso map to plan our day and get a sense of where we were. We sometimes ended up going the length of a country in the wrong direction.

Taipei in Taiwan was just a poor shantytown of wood, paper and tin houses. We got a bus around the island which terminated at a makeshift restaurant 6,000 feet above sea level. We had a bite and then decided to walk the 4,000 feet up the mountain. At around 8,000 feet I lost my mind. I started to laugh uncontrollably and dance all over the place and went weak at the knees. Simon had to grab me and lead me back down.

At one point we were able to get a twenty-four hour visa into Burma. We arrived at Rangoon airport and as we walked across the tarmac there was a huge planeload of half-dead people walking beside us. I asked where they were from and they answered that they were on a two-hour stopover and that they had just flown twenty-eight hours from London and had another twenty-eight hours to Sydney. I think that's why I have never been to Australia. We had to stay in a government run hotel and quickly discovered that there was a helluva black market for money. We promptly hired two pedal rickshaws and raced around town getting exchange rates. Eventually we got a load of local money for five dollars, and then when we found we couldn't take it out of the country, we went back to the hotel and tried to spend it all on over-priced beer before flying on to Calcutta the next day.

We crossed the Khyber Pass into Afghanistan by local bus which was full of tribesmen. Today you see Afghanistan on TV every night. Back then our only point of reference was Jesus Christ and the way he was dressed in holy pictures, so to us it was like being on a bus full of Jesuses. Many just wore huge white robes with half the world underneath: guns, suitcases, goats, bags of food, leather water flasks and bedding. Simon was smoking a lot of cigarettes in those days and so when a couple of men offered him a smoke, he accepted gracefully in the name of experience. After smoking a couple of the lads' cigarettes Simon said, "Steve, I know you don't smoke but this is unusual; I think you should give it a go." So I did and the two of us arrived in Kabul as high as kites. The tribesmen thought this was very funny and so invited us both to dance at the Muslim wedding they were going to. We said we had to find the local doss house first and they replied that we could stay with them. A bit nervous that we might have no bags or passports the next morning, we found a bed. I passed out but Simon went and danced at the wedding and was treated like royalty. First thing the next morning, I went out and got myself one of those Afghani flat top felt hats, a *pakol*, which looks a bit like those worn by English page-boys. It wasn't until I got back to England and talked about this strange tobacco to an unbelieving friend that I learnt the truth. He just couldn't believe how uncool I was.

From Istanbul, Simon was asked to drive a sports car with no clutch back to London in five days, which he did as he hadn't seen his girlfriend in Ireland for over two years. I hitched on once the Greek border opened. It had closed for a few days when the Generals took over the country on 21st April 1967.

Looking back, it seems like we left a trail of disaster after us as everywhere we went blew up after we left: terrible typhoons in Okinawa, war in Vietnam, riots and an earthquake in Hong Kong, the Six Day war in the Arab countries and being held up getting into Greece because the Generals had taken over the day before. In Italy the river Arno flooded Florence shortly after I had been sleeping under the bridges there. S❀P

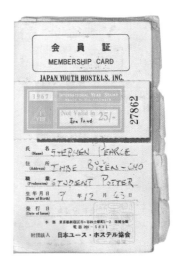

Above: My Japanese Youth Hostel card.

Below: The view from my window at Kaneshige Pottery.

ROCK 'N'
ROLL

"The boys are back in town."
Phil Lynott

I arrived in London in the middle of May 1967 and by chance met an old school friend, Tim Booth, in Finch's Bar on Portobello Road. In the school band I had been the singer and Tim the guitar player. While I had been away Tim and some pals had formed a band called Dr. Strangely Strange and he wanted me to manage them. I knew nothing about management but I suppose Tim knew that when I set my mind to something I always put a huge amount of energy behind it. Luckily, Tim had got to know a management company in London called Witch Season which had been very successful with The Incredible String Band. As the two bands had many similarities, I was able to see who liked the String Band and what made them successful. Both bands depended on the warmth of human contact and complete originality to get them through the night.

The first album circa 1964. Left to right: Tim Booth, Ivan Paule, Tim Goulding.

I first saw Strangelies after talking to Tim at a boat club on the Liffey where they were paid £15. (Just over a year later I booked them into Lisdoonvara Bachelors Festival for £750 for the night, although unfortunately I don't think the band ever made it.) Both Thin Lizzy and Strangelies used to come home and do a tour whenever the financial strain of trying to find a new audience abroad used up all of the cash. They both knew that they could sell out tours in Ireland, so they would come back home, build a little pile of cash, take a short break and then off to foreign, unconverted lands again. Rory Gallagher once told me that the reason why he focused so much on Germany was that you could earn the same money as in America with a fraction of the touring cost. Of course the master was Paul McGuinness. I was flying out of America with Freddy Laker one day when I met Paul in JFK airport. We sat in the back of the plane together and he told me about the tour that U2 had just finished – their first. What catches many Irish and English bands is that having done their first tour of America at great expense, if it's not quickly followed by a top ten single or album, no one is willing to pay for the next tour. So entry into this huge market is often blown. However, McGuinness, the old fox, toured the clubs and small concerts and then bigger concerts for three months with U2, so for minimal outlay he got a firm foothold in America all in one go. Well done Paul.

It was at Strangelies' first head-lining home tour which landed in University College Cork that I first met Isabel Healy. On the side of the stage sat Cork's foremost sculptor Seamus Murphy with the alluring, drop dead gorgeous bundle of fun Isabel on the floor by his feet. As the concert was in my hometown of Cork I headed off to a party with Martin Dwyer, Isabel and her friends. I was exhausted and left the party early. Fortunately, Isabel had noticed me and eventually joined me for a couple of years in London where she started her career as a journalist and writer. We have stayed good friends since and she has always supported me and the Pottery whenever she could. She is now a textile and conceptual artist herself, happily yarn-bombing sculptures

around the globe.

Packing a trolley of mugs for my turf-fired kiln in Shanagarry circa 1974.

While in England managing the band I supported myself by starting a small Pottery in the basement of my godmother Ruth Gill's house in London. I was using an English earthenware clay that was very unsatisfactory. Some of the shapes were much more unfocused and undirected than my usual pottery. I think I was so focused on the band that I was not fully with my pots. They were terracotta and white with just a little black and I used to sell them at The Irish Shop on Duke Street in London.

I had three godmothers which I must tell you about. First, Mary Gowing who treated me like a prince. When Mary died I elected Ruth Gill. Then, one night when I was staying with the cookery writer Margaret Costa at her central London flat, I arrived in late and she kindly asked me what I would like to eat. I said crab pâté, and I'm not having any of that 'bought stuff'. She promptly set to and made me an exquisite pâté for which I made her my godmother number three. Knowing Margaret, there was a nice little scoop of brandy in the pâté. I came back to the flat on another evening and all the way up three flights of stairs there was pre-packed food. I said, "What the hell is going on?" She said, "I forgot to tell you that I have been hired by Marks & Spencer to set up a food department and these are some samples that we have to taste." It went on for weeks. I have to admit there were quite a few things that never made it to our mouths. Then one day Margaret came home almost in tears. All she could say was, "They are so stupid those accountant men. They think food is like their cheap, ill-fitting clothes. They don't understand. They hired me to do something special and now all they want is another ordinary supermarket." I must say that my own experience of being a consultant is very similar. People come to me looking for my advice or design talent. They tell me how clever I am and that I am the only person whom they think can fulfil the brief and that it is going to be top of the range and break new ground and it will be great for my CV. Then along come the bean counters and mediocrity reigns. The only answer is to start day one with "Show me the money."

The reason Margaret was so upset was that she had gone to a lot of trouble sourcing and cooking free-range chickens, and all that the 'suits' had said was that they could buy chickens more cheaply. I don't know what happened after that, but Marks & Spencer's food is excellent and they have done exactly what Margaret set out to do. I would like to think that it had something to do with her Irish fighting spirit. After all, she was Maggie Murphy from West Cork who was scratched out of the family bible for marrying a non-believer.

My real godmother though was Ruth Gill. Ruthie was a very talented designer who chose to work in advertising in London. She put together, with her team in Mather and Crowther, some great campaigns: "Go to work on an egg", "Drinka pinta milka day", "Cream makes it better". The photography in the late fifties was the fore-runner of Marks & Spencer's food photography today. Her main man in the group was Roger Phillips who went on to break all sorts of new ground in photography and has since produced incredible plant books. Roger is now a world authority on roses and was the designer of medieval gardens for me some years later at Penn Castle in Shanagarry.

Ruthie lived north of Camden Town on the

Early Shanagarry invitation to Brown Thomas exhibition. Designed by Ruth Gill.

edge of Hampstead Heath just a skip and a jump from Sinead Cusack. (Years later when tobogganing on the heath I tried to make a match between my six year old daughter Lucy and Sinead's young fellah!) In total I spent years of my life staying with Ruth. She was a great cook, allowed me to start a Pottery in her basement and was quite forgiving. You know how the English have a phobia about rationing, train strikes, shortages, snow-blocked roads…? Well, once there was a threat of the water being cut off at Ruthie's house and she filled the bath with cold water so that we could make tea. After three days of no strike I said feck the water shortage, emptied the bathtub and had a bath. When she came home from work she nearly killed me.

Ruthie also introduced me to so many interesting people and things. People like the photographer Roger Phillips and Jock Kinnear who designed the English motorway signs, which were ground breaking at that time. Jock drew me a sign for the Pottery in his smart white letters on a blue background. I always thought it was gas to have a British motorway sign at the head of a boreen in Shanagarry. Later Jock started doing heritage type designs in brown and so I had the first road sign in Ireland in brown. Then I changed it to a deep red-brown like my terracotta. Now SuperValu and the Kilkenny Shop have copied that. What next? Remember when Darina Allen called her first book 'Simply Delicious'? Now you have Simply/Simple on everything. It's great to be first.

One day Ruth got a bill from her solicitor for minding her houses. She had six houses all in very good locations in North London. Her mother, who was married to a Protestant preacher, had somehow managed to buy the houses and gave them to Ruth. I went around to inspect the houses with an engineer friend. It was my opinion that she was being completely done by her solicitor, so I offered to manage them and make them profitable. Instead she went around and gave them to the tenants. At today's value they would be worth €8 million. Ruthie was always extraordinarily generous to me in many, many ways and when I was extremely lonely in Japan it was to Ruthie I turned and we wrote to each other almost every day. I suppose I was her son in a way as she never had children herself. I have noticed that the people who might make the best parents either don't marry or are gay. Maybe it's their freedom from the strain of kids that makes them more available.

Ruthie drew my S&P stamp (for Shanagarry Pottery or Stephen Pearce) as an Easter present while

I was an apprentice with my father. As it wasn't used much at Shanagarry it has come to represent me. My father always preferred his lead stamps which read 'Shanagarry' and 'Irish hand thrown'. Ruth liked to work very slowly and thoughtfully. Mary Gowing had interviewed Ruthie for her first job in advertising and her report read, "Miss Gill is so sweet but so slow." They became best friends and we often used to tease Ruthie that she was slow. I think it was Ruthie who encouraged me to make 7-foot high totem poles. I spent a year making and decorating five totems and Ruthie and I took them out on the lawn to photograph. Just as she had taken the photographs the wind blew them over and they were smashed to smithereens. Before I met Kevin Dunne, Ruthie used to photograph everything for me. Somewhere I hope there are boxes of her negatives.

When I joined Dr. Strangely Strange I had a two-year timeframe in mind. I wanted to be in London and I totally believed in the band, but I knew myself well enough that if I stayed too long I might become a drifter. London in the late 1960s was a blast. Music, new ideas, girls and all sorts of things and people... just the kind of life I wanted. I became an Arsenal supporter because a pal had a flat near their stadium and we would watch them on telly with the window open so we could hear the crowd cheering. I used to see Charlie George take off down the field with his long blond hair streaming out behind him, like a lion in full flight. There was so much: Hendrix, Richard Thomson of Fairport, The Grateful Dead, festivals, peace and love and brown rice in England and 'Zen Macrobiotic' in France. Our management office toured Frank Zappa and The Mothers of Invention in Europe. We played with Carlos Santana at the Lyceum in London. That concert was put on by the promoter John Smith, who was a good friend. Strangelies were second to the top of the bill and an unknown Elton John was opening. By the night of the concert Elton had a hit record. His manager came up to me and said that they were taking our place at second top. I said, "I'm not the promoter, let's talk to John." I winked at John and said this guy wants to change your running order. He winked at me and said, "Impossible. He either plays his spot or goes home." I really got to know 'Rockin' Ted

Photo with one of the original Totem Poles circa 1970. Photo Ruth Gill.

Ruthie's S❀P logo mark as it exists today.

Carroll of Chiswick Records well at this time as he was managing Thin Lizzy. At one point we were so sick of the record deals that we were being offered that I helped Ted start Chiswick Records. Both Strangelies and Lizzy got deals elsewhere and Chiswick went on to take over from the The Sex Pistols as the Punk focus.

There was a venue under Covent Garden called Middle Earth running all-night gigs with up to five different acts. They were always breaking new bands along with old favourites like Graham Bond, Peter Green and Pretty Things. One night Hendrix was jamming on stage. He had just arrived from America where any top manager could see that he would be trouble to manage. I was with a gang who wanted to record him because he was amazing. It was a mad idea. None of us wanted to manage Hendrix, but we figured that if a single was out there on the airwaves, someone would take him on. The rest is history. I saw his last London concert at the Albert Hall with our own Eire Apparent (a well-known Irish band in the UK at the time).

But it had to end. Unluckily, or luckily, Tim Goulding left our band and the boys decided to take on Gay and Terry Woods, which musically was a great idea. Gay had the voice of an angel but Terry had his own vision for the Strangelies and so things went downhill a bit. By this stage I owed a lot of money on the equipment and so I went back to pottery. It was a pity it ended in that way as it was all taking shape. Happily Tim eventually did come back to the band, realising that the combination of him with Tim Booth and Ivan Paul was something truly unique.

Whatever about my life in London, my travels to America at this time, where I went for inspiration, really blew me away. Even though I had travelled the world, it was extraordinary. The lack of subtlety is the first thing that struck me. The size of the cars, an immediate sense that you are in a military state, the attitude of the immigration officials, the parking police outside the terminal, the taxi drivers... there was a threatening aggression that I had never encountered before. In New York, there was a constant violent overtone: move along, don't stand there, don't ask me… so unlike European human chaos. It was like being at a circus with the madness of it all. It's definitely addictive and exhausting and not for me, even though I've had some great times there. I feel like a mouse in a crocodile swamp.

I spent my first night in New Canaan, Connecticut with the Geurreros. Pedro Guerrero had visited us in Shanagarry in the late 1950s to photograph my mother for the American *House and Garden* magazine and I had really liked him and, in particular, his daughter Susan. I'll never forget the breakfast with the strange orange juice, bacon and waffles, and that Ben, their son who was maybe eighteen then, had a red Ford Mustang outside the door. Two days later, I went down to New York to Port Terminal where the Greyhound buses gather. It was like a combat zone. The bus drivers were so aggressive they thought they were army generals. I love travel and, having done Siberia, crossing America was like a walk in the park. I would travel by night on the Greyhound buses to save money and stop off maybe twice a day for two to four hours per stop to visit random places. I enjoyed Chicago, Montana at dawn and dusk, the strange food, the bustling Greyhound stations, the strange smell in the toilets. At one small town the sheriff put two hippies on the bus. He had shaved their heads because he didn't like long hair. I went into a long, old-fashioned bar on a dusty boardwalk in a small, mean town and ordered a beer and the old guy, straight out of a Clint Eastwood movie, said, "We don't serve no hippies." I saw the first night of *Easy Rider* in San Francisco in July 1969. Soon after I was hauled off the bus in Texas by a sheriff and the guys were really rough until they saw my Irish passport. No apology though. I stopped in at Salt Lake City, Reno, Nevada, Tijuana Mexico and New Orleans. New Orleans was extraordinary. The food was different and the music outstanding, and I met an amazing girl. On my last day in New Orleans, I was walking along a big, wide street in the bright sunshine, stony broke, with my hair below my shoulders, an old Irish Free State army jacket and multi-coloured bell bottom jeans, when I passed a bank called Morgan Guarantee Trust. I thought, "Wow, I thought that bank only existed in New York and Washington." It was a bit fancy and as it happened I knew the president. So I went in (as one does when you're broke) and asked to see the manager. I said to tell him I was a friend of his boss. I explained to the manager that I was a friend of the president, Tommy Rodd (who happened to have a house in Fermoy). I explained that I had lost his number and needed to speak to him urgently. He rang New York and got Tommy on the phone. I told Tommy my situation and passed the phone back. The manager asked how much I needed, I said to give me $100. He said Mr Rodd said he could give me up to a $1,000. I replied no, $100 is fine. The manager said he would have liked to have bought me lunch if he hadn't already had an engagement, that I seemed like a really neat guy. I said thanks, put the money in my pocket and headed back out on the street.

Up along the East Coast there had been a fierce hurricane. As someone used to building with concrete blocks, I have never had much time for timber houses, especially right beside an ocean. Every house was flat, like bread waiting to become a sandwich. I got back on the bus one morning somewhere in Texas and sat beside a small black man in a denim boiler suit. We were passing miles of what looked like white puffy flowers. I asked my neighbour what sort of plant was out there. I thought maybe he was hard of hearing because he didn't answer until I asked him the third time. "Them's cotton," he said and I realised that he had thought I was some smart assed white kid trying to torment him. I explained that I was from Ireland "where we don't have no cotton" and we got on great after that and both learned a lot.

I stopped off in Norfolk, Virginia to visit Paula Fitzgerald, whose husband Edward was creative director of the movie *The Magnificent Seven*, and who had taught me to meditate, and maybe even levitate, many years before. Until I saw Virginia, I had always thought that peanuts or monkey nuts grew on trees, but no they were harvesting them with a machine much like an Irish potato harvester. When I got back to New York after 8,500 miles and thirty States (way more than most Americans have seen) there were still four days to go on my ticket, so I gave it to a friend to go to LA and it was bye, bye America. **S&P**

BACK HOME

Left to right: Philip, my sister Sarah, your man and Simon with Simon's dog Django. Photos (above and previous page) Ruth Gill.

"Expect change, welcome change, enjoy change."
Stephen Pearce

When I got back to Shanagarry in 1969, Simon was in full swing making pots there. I had got to the point where I really needed to express myself through my own pots and even though I behaved badly towards my mother, I didn't want to leave home. I think I took out a lot of my frustration on Simon. I started to build a wood-fired kiln in the garden and envisioned myself making a few of my own pots in my little workshop and working part time with my father. I really wanted to work on my own though.

In 1970 Simon eventually headed off to Bennettsbridge in Kilkenny and Philip gave him £5,000 to get started. Simon set up a small Pottery in a room of the old farmhouse that he had bought. His real passion at the time however was glass, but he needed to make pots while he planned how to do that and he needed to eat. I used to look forward to visiting Simon at the weekends. I admired what he was doing and loved seeing his new buildings and ideas. I really enjoyed simply hanging out with him and in those days there were some great little bars in the middle of nowhere in county Kilkenny. It was good of him to have me after I had been so difficult in Shanagarry. I will always be grateful to Simon for bearing with me and for forgiving me my difficult side.

After working with my father on and off for eight years I was driving us both mad. We had created the beginnings of an Irish Design/Craft Movement. The pottery was selling well and was regarded as the Irish Design/Craft item soon to be recognised by an International Design survey. However, I needed oxygen and my father needed peace of mind. I saw the same family drama played out in the homes of many local farmers where the father wanted the son to follow in his footsteps and the son wanted to trade in the Ford Dexta and a two-board plough for a monster that could pull a four-board plough and a bailer, a beet harvester and combine, as well as a huge hay shed and a milking parlour. For men who had known the de Valera era and never borrowed money, this was terrifying. Many young farmers with the same feelings as myself emigrated. For me it was easier. A Pottery only needs a small shed and a small investment in equipment.

Philip and Lucy soon realised themselves that I had outgrown living at home. I think that although I was a wild man, a part of me was terrified to leave home. It felt so safe; plus the food was out of this world. So Philip made me the same offer as Simon, with the addition of a piece of his land to build on only a hundred yards from home. I built my house for £6,000 and then mortgaged it to build my own Pottery. Luckily concrete blocks were cheap, so I just kept building. I intended working on my own, which I had always yearned for, building and making everything myself – a habit long learnt from my parents who always got me to make anything we needed. However, I very soon got lonely and hired young Willie Kenneally to help me.

What I like about designing and putting up buildings for myself is that I feel much freer than when designing pottery. I can do what I like and if nobody else likes it, it really doesn't matter. When I am designing a plate it may well be still in production fifty years hence and so I like to get every small detail right, which can often take months and months of concentrated effort. Building a house is easy, apart from planning permission. I just build and try to keep one step ahead so that pipes and wires end up in the right places. There is no engineering in a two

Above: The pin-up boy for the Bank of Ireland calendar. That was the day I met Kevin Dunne.

Below: The foundations for my house in 1971. I planted the trees in the background when I was eleven years old.

or three-storey house, so I can put doors and windows where I like and I am very unlikely to get involved with overloading spans. This means that it is down to building with feeling and remembering that a house is for the people in it and not for showing off to the neighbours. It's the ethos that counts for me: space and light, natural surfaces, wood, linen, terracotta tiles and gentle lines. Spaces to live and breathe in and yet still be cosy with fireplaces for log fires, and big, soft, deep sofas.

In my childhood many of the farmhouses in Shanagarry were built of mud and stone and plastered with mud or lime mortar coated with years of whitewash. As farmers often plastered their own houses in winter, when it was too wet to work outside, the finish was very uneven and wavy. It's natural and easy, unlike modern walls, which are dead square and hospital-like. A house for me is a nest and should be cosy yet balanced with light and space. You can have good-sized windows but not too big because windows let in some heat in Ireland's limited summer but also a lot of cold in winter. If I want to see outside, I go outside and feel the weather. No north-facing windows in Ireland. When drawing a house I make sure that there is drinking water near me at all times and a loo. Having plastered the walls in wavy plaster, I generally find some plain, soft-coloured Spanish terracotta tiles and lots of natural unpainted wood. There is no uniformity of woods; I use elm, ash, walnut, cherry, beech, sycamore and evergreen oak. Whenever I see interesting trees being felled I try to buy one and keep and season them for up to ten years. If left outside for a few years, water makes its way in through the end grain, particularly with beech. This gives an interesting texture to the wood. I do carpentry a bit like I plaster or make pottery. Everything has a lovingly used feel to it. No sharp edges and few straight lines. Having built a house with lots of natural light and simple lines it is now just waiting for a few paintings, some pottery and a couple of pieces of innocent antiques from the likes of Mexico or Tibet. Horse blankets for curtains, natural linens to cover chairs and Simon's sparkling, lovingly crafted glass. That's how I do houses.

The building of my original Pottery, and more recently our Tea Room in Shanagarry, follows the same principles. It is homely and efficient for both potters and visitors. People are constantly commenting on the feel of the Pottery. Actually it's what I have not done that makes it special.

I had a very close friendship with my mother and a high regard for her judgement and therefore I consulted her on everything. She was one smart cookie and so I never passed up an opportunity to run things by her. When I wrote something I used as few words as possible. However, one day Lucy said to me, "You have to imagine someone arriving from another planet and reading what you have written, so be sure that what you write will be understood by everyone." No two people have the same mental wiring or experience of life, so it

Above: Building my house, views of a working man and below, the finished product.

Opposite: Finally a bit of peace and quiet (post divorce).

Above: On the steps of Kilmahon, my godmother's rose bushes in full bloom. Guess how old I am here?
Opposite: In a rush to get the shillings coming in. The shop was open before the sign was painted.

is often useful to set a context before saying something. The trick is to keep the context short.

Just as I am about to leave home and start my own Pottery in 1973, my mother dies. I remember being offered my second pint after the funeral and wondering if it was disrespectful to my mother to get drunk. Then I wondered if it would be better to wake in the morning with a hangover or the pain of my loss. Strangely, almost immediately after my mother died, I had a closer relationship with her than I did in life. With all of the everyday stuff stripped away, I was able to have a much simpler, loving relationship. I believe my mother had chosen the timing of her death to coincide with my starting out on my own as her way of saying, "You're on your own now". She was letting me go so that I could fully move on with the next part of my life and become a man (which I forgot to do).

In the early 1970s emigration from Ireland was still very painful and there wasn't much chance of Ireland moving forward when the nation was crippled by unemployment. Compelled by all of this I started hiring people. My twin objectives were to make beautiful, simple and useful pottery and to employ as many people as possible. So in the summer of 1975 I planned a huge launch for my Pottery as one thing I had learnt in the rock 'n' roll business was PR. I had TV, radio, newspapers and magazines coming from everywhere to the opening. The day before, Justin Keating, who was Minister for Industry and Commerce at the time, kindly agreed to do the official opening but rang at the last minute and told me that de Valera had just died. We both knew that that meant no press. He asked me what I wanted to do. "It's too late to stop now. Let's just have a blast." And so we did. Marion Fossett sang her heart out till six in the morning and the story got one column inch in *The Cork Examiner*. Eventually, Ireland got over the loss of de Valera and journalists started ringing to see what they had missed. Justin also made a TV documentary about the pottery.

My Pottery opening party was amazing. There seemed to be hundreds and hundreds of friends and well-wishers. We had a bar with three taps on it and cases and cases of wine, three large bonfires with people sitting around and chatting and two or three bands playing.

Then the real work started. I really wanted to make a few pots in the same spirit as those which I had admired so much in Japan and France, but I couldn't believe that anyone in Ireland would want them. They were just shapes, not particularly useful, a bit wobbly, unsymmetrical and with textured surfaces. The thing about the pottery road that I have chosen is that it is very disciplined and at times I want to break loose. I also want it all to fit together. Being a man and competitive, this is how I saw my road: I had spent almost ten years helping my father's Shanagarry Pottery become one of the most prestigious design brands in the country and now I had to beat that without copying or being close to it. I was working away on the wheel and, as I was using the same Youghal clay as my father, I started using the same white glaze. I was glazing a pot. I had a jug of glaze in my right hand and a tall beaker in my left hand. I filled the beaker with glaze and poured it out and suddenly my style was born. What I had liked about the French and Japanese pots that I had worked with was the plain unglazed clay to hold in the hand. For me it is a real connection with something important and fundamental. When I saw that all I had to do to fulfil my dreams was to take the black off the outside, I burst out laughing. Talk about simple. I left that first beaker white inside the rim and raw clay on the outside so that when I drank from the beaker it was very sensual to me as my top lip caressed the white glaze on the inside while my lower lip experienced the roughness of the naked earthenware clay on the outside. By showroom sales I quickly realized that the people of Ireland weren't quite ready for this experience and so I glazed the outside of the rims in white, which I still do and which is another experience.

I was very much in love with the smooth finish of the creamy white glaze against the rough texture and colour of the terracotta, which varies so interestingly depending on the firings and position in the kilns. It just seemed so perfect. I didn't really expect anyone else to pick up on it and awareness in Ireland was still bubbling under the surface. Occasionally, an international designer would walk in the door and buy and rave about my pots and I felt very supported by them. It affirmed for me my determination to go on making my terracotta and white. I took very seriously the challenge to make pots that would not chip easily; that's why all of the early pieces have chunky rims and no sharp edges anywhere. I have become a bit more cheeky lately, having come across a few early pieces with paper thin lips which I like very much. I intend making a few pieces with fine rims and it's up to you to mind them. S&P

MARRIAGE

"I have only two prayers. Thanks. Help."
Stephen Pearce

I met Alison Gavin at her sister's wedding in the mid-sixties. She was fourteen and I was twenty-four and she sat on the floor in a mini skirt talking to her friend while William Bennett (the flautist) and I showed off our male prowess by racing each other up the poles of the marquee. I fancied the hell out of her but I felt there was no point in trying to bridge the age gap. A few years later I met her at a Strangely Strange concert. Then she called in at Shanagarry whilst hitching around Ireland with a friend. At some point Alison changed her name to Francesca. She was at art school and started to visit Shanagarry during her holidays. We were married at the Quaker Meeting House in Cork by Alan Houghton and Daisy Swanton in August 1979. The signs of a storm brewing were all there but I didn't choose to read them. Pan Am airline had just brought in its first cheapo round the world ticket and you could stop off wherever you wanted as long as you kept going round in the same direction. For our honeymoon, we first went to my brother's wedding in New Jersey. Simon had met Pia McDonnell when Sybil Connelly had brought Pia's mother, Peggy, and a bevy of beautiful daughters to visit Simon's glass workshop in Bennettsbridge. Simon immediately enjoyed talking to Peggy which made the young girls think he was chatting her up, but it didn't take Pia long to realise that his eye was on her.

From New Jersey Francesca and I flew to San Francisco for a few days and a friend of Pia's took us on a tour of Russian restaurants. I bet you didn't know there is a whole area of Russian restaurants in Frisco. Next, it was on to Hawaii and then Japan where our daughter Lucy was conceived in a *ryokan* (a small, traditional Japanese inn) in Kyoto. We also visited Mr Imaeda, who had originally introduced me to Japan and who was now into his eighties. The Sakakibaras were as welcoming as ever. Kyoto,

Above: My engagement to Francesca Gavin.
Below: After the wedding, with my godmother
Ruth Gill seated behind our dog.

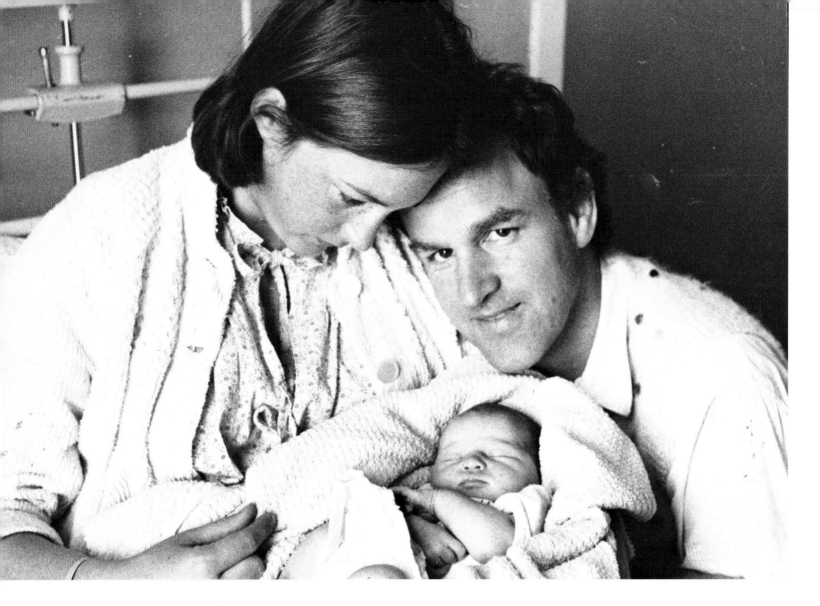

Lucy Pearce, 20th June 1980.

the middle brother, had become very famous since the 1960s and had built a beautiful house and mini golf course and had his own plane. The honeymoon continued with us stopping anywhere between Japan and Ireland. In June 1980, our daughter was born, named Lucy Helen after my mother. As I saw her little head peeping out my life changed. I had someone in my life who as and from that moment totally depended on me. I had not allowed for that. As most men are not that much into commitment, the sudden awareness that something totally non-negotiable in its exclusive intimacy is happening is at the very least terrifying.

Within six months we were getting divorced: a heart wrenching choice with Lucy so small. However, I felt sure that she was better off not living in a house with two parents continually fighting, and certainly I could not run a Pottery and fight with my wife. As to whether I chose well or not, only Lucy can say. It was years later that I came across a Buddhist wisdom: life is always changing. It is so true, yet we insist on trying to create stability. Tell that to a bird in a nest full of young ones on a stormy night. Many times I have found that that is the way life is, and still I resist it.

So what went wrong with our marriage? I suppose I was so focused on our love affair that I missed all of the little details around our characters and compatibility. I was really in love with Francesca and it was a wonderful time and she is a wonderful person. For me, it just didn't work as a long-term relationship: nobody's fault. For my part, I was incapable of making it work. I was spurred on to divorce by the conviction that our daughter would be far happier living in two peaceful households than on a battlefield. I am extremely grateful for the possibility of divorce in our society as I think the choice should rest with the couple and not the Church or State. However, I would not wish the choice on anyone. Divorce is horrible and always leaves blood on the tracks. Unfortunately, we have to go through the dark to find the light and mostly we come out wiser and stronger. Onwards and upwards there is light, always. **S♣P**

THE SHOP MAN

"I am not a businessman, but an educator by example."
Stephen Pearce

By 1982 I was officially divorced. I spent a lot of time in London during the two years prior to this, working with and learning from a man called Robert Daubigny. He ran seminars once a month and mini ones in between. The seminars were his take on 'est' (Werner Erhard's workshops in the human potential movement). The bottom line was that we are all totally responsible for everything in our lives, which, when you are getting divorced and blaming your partner, is pretty powerful stuff. I remember one evening Robert came into a seminar and said, "I have something I would like to share with you. It is my definition of forgiveness: to forgive is to let go forever the right to revenge." Anyone who thinks that they have forgiven anyone for anything should look carefully at this definition.

Bridget O'Riordan joined us in late 1982 and went on to do an amazing job holding the Pottery together. Of all the people who have worked with me in Shanagarry over the years Bridget was probably the most important. Having joined us to work in the office she ended up running the complete Pottery. When I look at the top ten, (and there were at least ten great names), Bridget comes out on top mainly because she was way smarter than me. I never needed to explain anything to her, nor check up on her and she brought so many ideas of her own. She was young and cranky when she arrived but then so was I. She took no prisoners so I had to watch my step and I always felt very safe when Bridget was around minding the money. Maybe when she is finished in the supermarket business I'll persuade her to come back.

Back in the early 1980s, Bridget had to do a whip-round to pay for the phone and electricity, and the tension of expanding built as the banks still weren't lending, not to me anyway. Then one day I went to buy a wood-fired stove from an old acquaintance, Jim Canning. Jim fancied himself as a kind of an accountant. He was advising farmers on their tax and doing liquidations (hence the wood-fired stove). For a reason that I can no longer remember, Jim persuaded me to sit into the car and drive to Galway with him.

Jim was an unusual man. I was never very keen on him when we were kids because he seemed to be all show and very pushy. He and his father Bill along with his mother Grace all worked for my uncle Brian on his farm near Lismore in Co. Waterford. As a child on cold wintery days I had spent many wonderful hours with Bill chopping kindling in the dark barn that smelt of creosote and was lit with an old kerosene Tilley lamp. There was another older shed where, after the cows with their young calves had been inside for the winter months, there might be two feet of manure to clear out. I would sit on a manger and Bill would tell me stories while he cut the manure out with a silage knife. I remember the strong, deep, earthy smell of silage manure mixed in with the smell of the Nuffield tractor, which my uncle had bought because he admired Lord Nuffield. It was a mountainy farm and there were always patches of gorse to be cleared and I would often go with Bill as he worked and watch the rabbits run for new cover as the gorse disappeared. If my uncle was away I might go home with Grace and spend the night in their cottage. Grace also used to bath me in a zinc tub in front of the open fire along with my cousin Robin. I took against Jim after I saw him kissing Robin behind the hen house one day when I was about ten and Jim five years older than me. Then he started treating my uncle's tractor roughly. Eventually Jim went into selling second-hand cars and then, when nobody would insure him any longer, he went to England. There Jim dressed like a Teddy Boy, all slick with drainpipe trousers, and sold sewing machines door to door. Jim was a great bullshitter and did very well. I don't know if it was at his office or while selling a sewing machine that Jim met a good-looking girl called Kay who came from a totally different social background to him. Maybe from where she was the guys were a bit dry; she found Jim exciting and gave him his big break. Later when Kay's parents died she kindly gave Jim her inheritance which is what got him started in Ireland.

With that under our belt let's get back into the car on the way to Galway. At this point Jim had a mansion and a large farm outside of Naas. My finances were on a knife edge as I had not been focused on the Pottery whilst dealing with my divorce. I was still expanding and I had developed a terrible ulcer as a result of the previous five years. We were driving along, going around a corner when Jim said to me, "You know I could help you sort out the Pottery." It was like a sound from heaven. Every hour I was having these terrible stomach cramps and life really wasn't much fun. We talked and I learned that in Jim's formative years my uncle had been like a father to him, which is an instinct that my father, my brother and I all share. We want to see everyone happy and fulfilled in their lives. I remember that in 1971, when I built Paddy Fitz's house for him, my father insisted on paying for it so that Paddy wouldn't have the burden of a mortgage. The house cost £2,500.

Naas shop interior.

Jim really aspired to being a part of our family. He seemed to really care about my difficulties and really believed that the pottery could be much more successful. He started doing my accounts and was very keen for me to get out of debt, so I worked on it for a while. Jim wanted to open a chain of shops with my name over the door and so we bought a shop from him under his office in New Row, Naas in Co. Kildare. As computers at this time were just getting started Jim agreed with my idea that we should link the shop till to Jim's office computer. That way we could learn really quickly who bought what and when and how much stock we should hold, and of course the margins. It never happened as Jim was great at putting ideas together but not interested in the nitty gritty of following up. My dream was to open four major stores in Ireland, then franchise to people all over Ireland, then the United Kingdom followed by Europe and America. For this we needed clear bottom line analysis, which of course we never got.

I designed the fittings for the Naas shop. There were shelves and pottery racks of simple but solid wood on the walls and units, a little lower than table height, with pinewood doors and pottery stacked near to where it was displayed. It was predominantly stocked with my pottery and just a little of my father's, as he was headed for eighty years old at this stage. Of course there was a good display of my brother's glass as there always is in all of my shops. I really enjoy having the whole family together. The floor was laid with terracotta tiles, the walls and ceiling were white with natural wood fittings. There were vibrant coloured woollens, beautifully turned wooden bowls by Ciaran Forbes and Liam O'Neill and the glitter and reflections of Simon's glass. We had jewellery by Jennifer Hudson, children's toys by her daughter Tiggy and the shop was run by the serious, friendly and smiling Cathy Duff. What I remember about all of my shops was the colourful sparkle and the smell of coffee and woollens. There was a modern, comfortable, homely atmosphere and people loved it.

Jim was great at getting his hands on money. I once said to a banker, "If Jim comes in and fills you full of lies and you know they are lies, you give him the money. If I come in and give you as clear a picture as possible you give me nothing." The banker's retort was, "Jim is a smart man. He understands business."

Going around Cork city one day in the early 1980s with shops in mind, I saw a wonderful old disused warehouse in Paul Street. It was in an area that dates back to the 1700s, a Huguenot quarter with long, old winding lanes but which had been lying empty and unused with hoardings and was not very safe. The building was of red brick with limestone sills and a simple curve over each window. I just wanted to own it. The building spoke my language and would be a comfortable home for the pottery in my home town. I also felt that it would give me the right sort of presence in Cork. Paul Street had the reputation that nothing would ever succeed there. I knew I could and was aided and abetted by *The Cork Examiner* which printed a series of interesting articles on what appeared to be the only man with hope for Cork's future. Unfortunately, the poor man who owned the Paul Street building was going broke. When I went to the auctioneers, the whole building which extended between French Church Street and Carey's Lane and from Paul Street to the back of the Ulster Bank on Patrick Street, was for sale for €150,000. I signed the paperwork and gave the auctioneers a cheque for £5,000 and told them that I had no money so to hold the cheque. I rang Jim and he said he had no money but that he would talk to the auctioneer. The deal was done.

As I wanted to restore the area I was interested to know what City Hall's position might be on it. A very dear and supportive friend, Donal Musgrave of *The Cork Examiner* kindly introduced me to the visionary City Manager, Joe McHugh, who was of enormous support. We worked well as a team. One day Joe came into the shop looking very down and out and said to me, "I want you to take a walk with me." We went over to the English Market and Joe explained that he was under serious political pressure to redevelop it as a multi-storey car park. At that time the market was going downhill. I said to him, "Joe, you have done a lot for Cork but this is the most important choice of your tenure. This must stay." We went for a pint and he said, "I will start doing it up slowly because I won't get much money as long as it is thought possible to make it a car park." He did go ahead and when he got more than half way through the refurbishment people started to use it more. It was one of those times where he did the right thing at the right moment.

A few years later Joe invited me for a pint up by Shandon. By this time Joe was running Bord Gáis and Tommy Rice was City Manager. When I walked in to the bar and I saw that Joe, Tommy and the man from the Enterprise Board were sitting there I knew I was in serious trouble. For years the Enterprise Board had been trying to make a go of a wonderful, old, cut stone building as a craft centre and were seeing that their money and energy would be better used on other projects. Joe asked me would I take over the building. It was a very exciting project and I was totally flattered. Joe could see me faltering though and asked me what the problem was. I replied, "Mainly because I have this wonderful new girlfriend who has come down on the train from Dublin for the weekend and she is sitting waiting for me in Arbutus Lodge". Another pint arrived and another. I finally extracted myself and left half of the last pint and headed off to meet Lauren, my soon-to-be second wife. My dilemma over the project was that I had a lot of debt on the Cork shop, a Galway shop was about to open and I had lots of ideas that I wanted to bring to fruition in the Pottery. I also needed to put up a new building and I sensed that my relationship with Jim Canning was going to end. So this was another project I did not need even though it sounded like winning the lotto.

When I got to Arbutus, Ireland's first Michelin starred restaurant and my favourite, Lauren had been taken under the wing of two young British business men who had seen this orchid languishing all on her own and invited her to join them for "shampoo". How could people who invented the English language be so naff? Shampoo turned into an invitation to dinner and by the time I arrived they were on cheese and vintage dessert wines. As I went into the dining room, patron Declan Ryan looked at me as if to say, "Now Pearce, dig yourself out of this one if you can!" The English, gentlemen to the end, ordered a main course for me and I suppose went on to more shampoo. I bet they were wondering why such a beautiful woman would be involved with a drunk who turns up three hours late? Well done to Lauren's incredible generosity of spirit and understanding. Years later we met the same two guys in Arbutus again and they couldn't believe we were still together.

In 1984 when I started construction on Paul Street, nothing was happening in Cork. Traditionally, Cork had been run by a group of about ten merchant princes. There were the Dwyers who ran Sunbeam Wolsey the clothing factories in Cork, Midleton, Youghal and more. There were Thompsons' bakeries, Clayton Love fisheries and supermarkets, Beamish, Crawford, Murphy, Roche and Crosbie. These families were the brains and wealth of Cork. By the mid-1980s, they had run out of steam for the moment. Most of the main street, Patrick Street, was for sale and I was going to buy it with American backing through my brother. My only obstacle was that after several attempts I failed to find an estate agent who could write a report that made numerical sense to the Americans so that it would be a deal. The four main properties on the street were available for less than half a million pounds. My own property, bought for £150,000, was worth €40 million in less than twenty years, although I was long gone from the partnership by then. Was I smart? No. I was innocent, naïve – and lucky?

Before buying the Paul Street building I rang my friend Hugh Coveney, the politician and structural engineer and asked him to meet me in Paul Street. I asked him, "You have recently been mayor of Cork. Is there a highway planned to go through this area?" He said no. I then asked, "As an engineer, is this building about to fall down?" He said no. "Then why is nobody interested in buying it?" I asked. He answered, "Because a developer would demolish it and put up a new steel and glass structure, and in the present climate the numbers wouldn't stack up." I asked him what he thought of my plan and he replied, "I think it's a great idea for Cork and, if you're lucky, you shouldn't lose money." So I bought it.

Before proceeding with my plan to restore the site I needed to know what City Hall would say. Joe McHugh, myself and the chief fire officer hiked it down to the building and into the dusty gloom. I asked the fire officer whether he would insist that I cover the wonderful wooden beams in plaster and he got out his ruler. As the beams were twelve inches square pitch pine he said that they could remain exposed as once fire burnt in a certain amount it would starve of oxygen and leave enough structural integrity for the beam to hold its load. Next, Bill Reidy the city engineer had to approve joining the ground and first floor windows, which I wanted to do in order to create light and spectacle, but thereby throwing the total load of the building on to the narrow columns between the windows. Bill smoked a Sherlock Holmes pipe, said very little and thought a lot. He knew a lot about the history of Cork buildings and listening to him I almost forgot the purpose of my visit. Bill explained to me that historically Cork was known as the Venice of the West due to there being more waterways than roads. In fact, the city was built on a series of islands surrounded by the River Lee as evident in a map from the 16th century. Eventually the waterways between the islands were built over and now form some of the present day main streets. Many shops in Cork city still have the right to moor a boat outside the door in their title documents. Paul Street was a fairly poor area and to construct the original building on my site it had been necessary to drill long oak piles into the river mud in order to put up a building. Bill's concern was that if you alter the way the building is loaded on the piles, what would happen? I went off and found an engineer who did the calculations and went back to Bill. We had another great chat and Bill said for me to return in a week's time. He approved the plans but was most concerned that a wonderful wrought iron staircase was being taken out of another building and if somebody like me didn't rescue it for posterity it would be sold for scrap iron. I didn't have the time. About two years later, Bill rang me to say that the City needed to take down a wonderful old stone façade and would I take it, I went and looked and told him the City would just have to keep it as it was very much part of Cork. Now it stands proudly in front of the park on Grand Parade just beside a part of the old city wall. Hundreds of people a day pass through it and on some level enjoy it and are linked to history. Looking back, it is unbelievable how little money City Hall had for projects in the 1980s, and yet they had great vision.

Joe McHugh was an extraordinary force for progress in Cork; quite exceptional. He nurtured people like myself and Owen O'Callaghan. In fact, the Paul Street car park, the first multi-storey in Cork, was built by Owen at Joe's insistence way ahead of its time. The city also built several new bridges, the first in over a hundred years. Joe had a remarkable team around him and if they had had a bit of money even more remarkable things would have happened. One of Joe's great ambitions was to pedestrianise Patrick Street. He knew what a hot potato it would be and that it must be done slowly, over time. I always suspected that one reason for not allowing a multi-story car park to gobble up the English Market was that it would make the argument for pedestrianising Patrick Street that much more difficult; who knows? Joe must have been good because he has left a legacy of jealousy that so far has prevented myself and Owen from erecting a monument in his honour. I have a lovely piece of pure white marble standing by for it in Italy. It is over two metres high and comes from the same mountain where Michelangelo quarried the stone for his famous David. (Interestingly, Michelangelo had similar problems with the Church before completing his dream.) I am not going to do a statue of Joe, but rather what I see as a symbol of the progress he created.

In the centre of my Paul Street building I erected a huge central column. This was a stairwell and

lift shaft. However, with the number of holes that were being knocked in the rest of the building, I felt that I needed something really solid right up the centre of the building to tie it all together. My engineer put an insane amount of steel in the foundations. I had never worked with steel foundation cages but luckily Joe was building the Christy Ring Bridge so I asked could I watch for an afternoon. After an hour the steel fixers said to me, "You don't want to try doing this, it's hard, dirty work." And they were right. However, they kindly came over on a Saturday and set up my steel. At the time I had the biggest shop windows in Cork. The glass company and the city fathers all told me that in that run down area I was going to get vandalised and that I should put up shutters. Despite all the evidence to the contrary, I have a lot of faith in mankind. It seemed to me that if you brighten up a slum the first people to benefit are the passersby. Indeed, the windows were broken three times, after which I got Peter McNiff from RTÉ to come down and cover the development for his current affairs programme after the nine o'clock news. Over a coffee he confided that while he was happy to do the story, he thought it would be like a red rag to a bull. I replied that I would take my chances and believe it or not I never had another broken window. I don't begin to understand why.

The Cork shop was a large fresh idea. Nobody in craft was doing very well in the mid-1980s and I was the first to open a big, bright, colourful shop showcasing the best of Irish design and craft. We consciously filled the gaps with as few imports as possible. I was the first in Ireland to give Bewley's coffee to everyone who came in; Jim was always complaining that it cost four cent a cup. Big deal. To me making someone feel welcome was more important. Some Easters I would put a hen and her chicks in the window, another year it was rabbits. I saw the shops partly as an educational museum where people could come and browse at their ease and be exposed to new ideas. Once, in the plaza in front of my shop in Paul Street, I put a 30-foot ESB pole in a barrel of sand and stabilised it with boards from the third floor window. I gave plywood and paint to the crowds of kids we had invited and climbed the pole with spiked boots that the ESB kindly lent me and nailed the children's paintings all over the pole like a totem.

I have always enjoyed doing up old buildings. The shop in Paul Street was particularly wonderful to do as with a simple classic warehouse exterior I was able, by joining the ground and first floor windows, to have six, almost 20-foot columns, of natural light flooding into the shop. The light-filled space you entered into was two-storeys high with a balcony facing you, which itself covered about a third of the floor space. We sand blasted all of the huge old beams and stone corbels that held them and then we simply painted the interior brickwork, laid down high-fired terracotta tiles and we were away. It was quite an experience entering the shop. From the outside, which faced onto the main plaza of the area, you got very little warning of the colour, light and airy space which was about to hit you. The coffee was free, the staff were friendly and on the case and it was like a treasure trove. I definitely am proud of what we achieved. People gave me credit for leading the rejuvenation of Cork at a very dark time. Sometimes it's good to be innocent. Having bought the whole block between Carey's Lane and French Church Street we decided to look for people who would open interesting stores to buy and lease the shops from us. Con Collins opened a wonderful bookshop, then Michael O'Callaghan opened a wild bistro called The Huguenot. There followed twelve to fifteen more stores including little cafes, interesting clothes shops and an avant-garde jewellery store. We had also planned a huge art gallery and a contemplative garden on the site of the old Huguenot graveyard. Joe McHugh then pedestrianised the area and so it was that Cork's most ethnic and buzzing area was born.

Next Galway, which we bought from father and son duo, the Corbetts. This was a huge premises on Eyre Street. Jim and I went up to Galway to the offices of the solicitors who were also father and son and probably in their sixties and eighties. There was a senior accountant from the Bank of Ireland, Canning and myself. Everyone started playing stupid out of date 'male' games. When it got to the point of Corbett's solicitor asking the Bank of Ireland to show him the cheque so that they'd know it really existed, the banker said they could see it, but in his hands only. I gave up. I said, "Guys, I have this strange affliction that I can only sign my name for ten minutes from time to time and I am in that space right now. So if you need me to sign anything put it in front of me now. Then, if you need me for anything else I'll be lying on the grass in Eyre Square with an ice-cream in my hand." Three hours later Jim came out and said to me, "You did the right thing".

Jim actually enjoyed that sort of male posturing and carry on. I enjoyed my strawberry and vanilla ice-cream in the warm afternoon sunshine. It says a lot about me too that I can remember the flavour of the ice cream and not the names of the people at the meeting. I think it's called prioritising your life.

When we did the Galway shop in 1988 it was huge. We had a space in the centre which had been a builder's yard and we had steel erectors to put in a double-storey section. Some areas of the shop retained two stories but the centre was left open to the full two-storey height with an enormous glass ceiling allowing the light to pour through the shop. The feel of the Galway shop was similar to Cork but a bit more spectacular. It had a hint of circus about it. I left a whole central section with just bare steel girders so that we could do extraordinary displays. I never design a shop to be smart. I do it like a film set, so that things can be moved around and I always have plenty of electrical power points. Unfortunately I don't think I have a single photo of Galway, but it was wild. I may well be the only Irish shopkeeper who has fun. The opening of the Galway shop really surprised me; I had thought that Galway would be fun, but nothing prepared me for the style in there. I would like to say that Galway women certainly go for it when they go for it.

At a time in Ireland when the economy was stagnant, it was a wonderful thing to see something happening. I would like to think we gave people hope of a brighter future, and it certainly was a bright shop. We were probably the first shops in Ireland with a bright modern outlook. We sold as much Irish design as possible and were responsible for helping kick-start a lot of small businesses.

I took great pleasure in designing the shops and showing carpenters how to make the fittings. In fact if I hadn't been a potter I would probably have been a carpenter. Pat Scott was on hand to help with space, colour, light and inspiration and as always helped to create a gracious and generous flow and feel to the spaces we built. I have never seen Pat stumped where an idea is needed.

The people of Galway were very good to me. I used to meet Michael D. Higgins in the street and I suppose we both believed in a positive future for Ireland when the evidence then was the opposite. He would thank me for opening such a beautiful shop in Galway (which is now the Corrib Centre).

Above: Caroline Canning smiling in the Naas shop. Below: With Jim Canning and exhibitions officer Kim-Mai Mooney.

The real hero of our shops was Caroline Canning, Jim's eldest daughter. She had some of her father's street trader qualities though I think she really wanted to be an artist, which she now is. Caroline took on the shops and very quickly had it figured out. She had a great ability to both listen and understand my design ideas and also make commercial sense of things.

Jim meanwhile could never stop thinking up new projects, a bit like me. The problem was that he really needed to get the whole structure of the shops nailed down, but instead he was off doing other things. Jim went to an auction in London one day and came back with a couple of sketchbooks of watercolours, some finished, some not by Mildred Anne Butler, an early 20th century landscape painter from Thomastown, Co. Kilkenny. He had the watercolours framed and put an exhibition of them together which toured Ireland starting in the Crawford Gallery in Cork and ending in the National Gallery in Dublin. Jim's whole scheme was to buy sketchbooks for very little, make a name for the paintings by showing them in prestigious state galleries and then sell them for as near €20,000 a piece as he could.

I went to the Press Reception for the exhibition in the National Gallery, which is very memorable to me for a different reason. It was where I met the love of my life: a story I will come back to later on.

Jim and I had some great times and I think that he was genuinely fond of me. What Jim called the 'tinker' in him was always there, and therefore the idea of properly focusing on the shops to take them to another level as I had dreamed, could never happen. I learned a lot from Jim. We had our similarities in that no scheme was too wild for either of us. For me everything must have integrity though, and it is important to respect the people around me, unless they treat me really badly.

I am grateful to Jim for helping me take the pottery to a greater audience. If he had stayed focused we could have done amazing things, but of course that was not his nature and I should have seen that. I suppose I was blinded by my vision. Jim was

Kid-friendly days in Paul Street.

cute but he wasn't clever. With an investment of about half a million over three years, we created a property portfolio which within a few years was worth nearly a hundred million.

The Galway shop opened in 1988 and after a while, a Carmelite building became a possibility in Dublin. I must have been brave, stupid or mad to take on all of these projects. My mother would have killed me. She always said, "Stephen, if you would only stick to one thing I know you would be very good at it." My response was, "But it was you who encouraged me to have endless imagination!" She would smile happily and stay quiet. Dublin was to open the following year on Clarendon Street beside Powerscourt Townhouse. While all of this was going on, in 1987 I was doubling the size of the Pottery with a new clay preparation area, proper offices and custom built kiln rooms. By this time Lauren and I were definitely an item and she introduced me to Barbara Dawson (who later became the director of the Municipal Gallery of Modern Art in Dublin) and her husband Paul McGowan. Paul being a top flight accountant, and one of the youngest ever to be made a partner at KPMG, has given me invaluable and solid advice ever since, some of which I have occasionally listened to! The friendship was forged sitting on a bale of straw, drinking pints at the opening of the new Pottery building in the summer of 1987.

Around this time, either Paul or Jim persuaded me to turn the Pottery into a limited company and so National Crafts trading as Stephen Pearce Pottery was born. Jim and I met up in London in 1989 and dissolved our partnership, with him taking the shops and me going back to my roots. I allowed him to go on using my name for a short while and then Stephen Pearce shops became House of James.

By then, I was in full flight. With all of my shops selling lots of pottery, our other outlets and retail customers began to sit up and take notice. They realised that if you display my pottery well and people can see it, then they might really want to buy it. I was the first serious craft design shop. Shops like Avoca, Meadows & Byrne and Marion O'Gorman with the Kilkenny Shop soon followed. Jim and I were the highest bidders on the original Kilkenny Design shop in Nassau Street, but the government

Above: Stephen up the pole entertaining.
Opposite: Liam Clancy in the Pottery entertaining.

thought better of selling to us.

I needed more production as demand increased and office spaces to deal with the corresponding increase in paperwork and management. So up went the building adjoining the Old Pottery that was going to solve everything. I also had a couple of acres next door and when Lauren took stock of how many families came to visit our Pottery, she suggested we plant a beech wood maze for the children to run around in. Lauren designed the maze and based it partly on Cork's Garryduff gold bird (a medieval pin full of Celtic swirls), in honour of the bird sanctuary at Ballynamona fronting the Pottery, and partly on a fish as we are also on the edge of Ballycotton Bay. For those who understand mazes there are apparently ways to figure them out, but Lauren studied the systems and put in three different twists to snooker the experts.

I really wanted to make the Pottery a family affair for the people visiting us, and Joe McHugh unwittingly provided the impetus. Cork city became 800 years old and Joe asked me to consider making a plaque that City Hall could give to dignitaries and guests who visited during the year. Driving home from talking to Joe I stopped in for tea with Hazel Allen at Ballymaloe and her gang were all asking when they could come over and make things with clay. We had also started taking our pottery wheel to six or eight events around the country, and there was great interest shown by parents in their children having a go at it. It had never occurred to me before how much children liked playing with clay. In those days in Ireland, children were told don't touch this or keep away from that, which was very natural for a nation of citizens nervous of expressing their own ideas and feelings and always assuming someone else was smarter than them. I was always cross at how our Irish education chose to ignore the inherent creativity in every child, and so I seized the opportunity. I told Joe that plaques weren't me and that I was flattered and grateful to be asked but that I was going to do children's Sunday afternoons instead. To drive my message home I called the Sundays 'Make your own Masterpiece',

Top: Gerald Pringle's Garryduff bird 1960.
Middle: Paths for maze before trees were planted. Photo Roger Phillips.
Below: The current Garryduff bird on a special edition plate.

suggesting that there is creative genius in each of us. Parents would drop off their children at three o'clock and then go off for two hours. When they returned, the children would show their parents how to make pottery for half an hour themselves. My idea was to reverse the roles for a short time so that the possibility of a new sort of relationship might take root. On another level, I wanted to give people the opportunity of reconnecting with that primordial relationship we have with clay. Plunging your hands into the silky smooth, wet clay taken from our own earth and experiencing the excitement there is in using and making things with it, is such a deep held, essential experience that I think we are drawn to it both as adults and children. Children have fewer inhibitions and are able to let themselves go. I find that parents seeing this allow their own excitement to bubble up and in turn lose their inhibitions and start to make their own master-pieces.

Whenever children came we would let them wander around the menagerie of an-imals that Lauren had gathered: hens, ducks, goats, donkeys and angora rabbits as well as the Pottery dog and cat. Many of the animals had been given to us precisely because friends knew we had families visiting and that the animals would be given a friendly home milling about the Pot-tery. I remember one little girl had never seen a hen nor knew that eggs came from hens. Lauren gave me a parrot, whom we called Harry Canary, for Christmas and the kids loved him. We had an angora goat and a crazy beautiful Silkie cockerel who used to go for walks with me. On Sun-days in the winter months, Lana, Gerald Pringle's wife and friend of my mother's, made delicious barmbracks which Nora Paul plastered with butter and doled out to all the visitors along with cups of tea. Nora, whose mother Joanie had minded me as a child, was the chief pottery glazer for years and was the only person whom my daughter Lucy would allow to wash her hair when she was little. If in doubt in the Pottery, ask Nora. She was like the Pottery Mother. The night we opened the new building, Nora was in charge of food. She had sides and sides of bacon and she carved them all herself. She was bent over with an electric carving knife, got especially for the occasion. When I asked, "How's it going?" She said, "Can't you see how it's going, the sweat is running off me!" I offered her a drink and she said no, "I'll finish here first."

She was great, and so is Sophie her niece. Sophie Lahive came to the Pottery to es-cape from school. She thought she was interviewing for the Pottery but she immediately became one of our family. We would lend her to the Pottery sometimes. When Lauren and I had our children Mirin and Oran, in 1991 and 1993, so Sophie got drawn to the centre of our family and was a huge part of their childhood experience. Sophie always said, "Now I don't need to have kids, I've done my bit for Ireland." We all know that nature isn't like that and so now she has her own Joshua and Barra, and is still an important part of our family. In fact they are a hard family to shake off. Sophie's elder sister Lisa joined the Pottery for a few years at this time of expansion and was one of our best kiln packers before leaving to have a family. (Now she is back twenty years later with her daughter Shelley and they mind our showroom, make delicious cakes and pies for the Tea Room and pack kilns and internet parcels. So from great grandmother Joannie to Shelley now it's been sixty-six years of friendship. I like the feeling of continuity in some things as long as there is the freedom to move on as well.)

Between our 'Make your own Masterpiece' weekends, the demonstrations we did and the school tours that came and still come, several tens of thousands of families started to have a much closer friendship with my pottery than simply buying pots. I could never have guessed that this would happen, but I suddenly found myself virtually part of all of these fami-lies, which was and still is very rewarding. **S&P**

THE CELEBRATION

"If someone treats you badly, don't be angry. Know that
if they knew better they would treat you better."
Ancient Buddhist saying

In 1988, two farmers' wives (well one farmer's wife and the wife of a man in the chicken business) came to see me to invite me to a meeting in nearby Gortroe. Margaret Browne and Joan Vaughan were heading a group from Killeagh and Youghal to try to stop an American pharmaceutical plant being put right in the middle of a rich milk producing area with rolling green fields stretching all around. The Irish government had spent a lot of money creating a zone at Ringaskiddy in Cork Harbour especially for this type of plant. However, Merrell Dow didn't want to be there as they didn't want to be associated with the sort of pollution that they said was, and still is, going on at Ringaskiddy. Merrell Dow was allowed to virtually stick a pin in a map and build there. The farmers were not going to tolerate it. Had the Merrell Dow plant gone ahead there were to be discharges into the river, which is one reason that it was chosen to be sited in that spot. The river discharge would have entered the sea about half a mile downstream just where salmon like to rest before or after spawning in the nearby Blackwater River. The dioxin pollution in the air was believed to enter the food chain via grazing cattle, eventually causing problems for pregnant women. I used to jog on Shanagarry strand in the early morning when chemical companies in Cork Harbour took to discharging airborne pollution in the small hours. When the wind blew from the south west, the stink on the beach was sickening. Given that I had my fingers in many pies at this time, word on the street was that I was good at getting things done and so I was invited to one of their meetings. I was outraged by what I heard and decided to become involved. I talked to Bridget and some of the Pottery crew, letting them know that I saw danger in what I was doing. Charlie Haughey was in power then, Fianna Fáil were very strong in our area and did not smile on any opposition to their plans however misguided they might be. I knew there was a possibility that I might lose my Pottery through some political skulduggery, but from a moral standpoint if we don't fight for the environment our grandchildren will have nothing. Indeed, the world wasn't as aware then as it is now of the delicate balance of coexistence of humans, plants and what the air and water carry to all of us. My passion was such that I gave a ten minute monologue on Kenny Live and appeared on Bibi Baskin's TV show, along with a mountain of other stuff on the radio and in the papers. What I remember best though was a phone call I received from RTÉ Radio one afternoon in September 1989 at about four o'clock when I was told that Merrell Dow was pulling out of Ireland. I burst into tears and sang 'A Nation Once Again' on the phone, which went out live on air.

The stupidity and lack of vision of some of our national institutions can only be marvelled at, as can those institutions worldwide. Can you believe that now, almost thirty years later, the Irish government is trying to make the people of Youghal accept the most toxic waste from Ringaskiddy? This waste will travel by road and pass by and through major areas of population to be processed in Youghal with the residue piped directly into the Blackwater River. The sort of pressure that fighting a campaign like this produces is incredible. You are up against central government, County Hall and some of the wealthiest companies in the world. It can be fought, and must be fought. I am afraid that I only had the energy for one such campaign. I fully support the people of Youghal in this fight and wish I had the energy to be on the frontline.

A lot was happening in the late eighties and I was feeling pretty good when I found time to check in on myself. My Pottery had been going for twenty-five years and so to mark the opening of the new Pottery building and the fact that things seemed to be going so extremely well, I launched the blue range and called it my Celebration range. It was the result of a couple of years of research and development with Philip Wood, a potter from Somerset and an expert on pottery glazes. Philip has been a friend and collaborator for years.

In the mid-1980s, many of the shops we supplied were asking for colour. Philip came over and developed some amazing colours: beautiful soft pastels in pinks, greens and blues. Though I liked them, I didn't feel they were me. He then developed an amazing range of very subtle pieces with individually made decorative sprigs depicting animals, birds and plants stuck all over the pots. I really liked them but the idea of having a team of 80 people collaborating on a project like that, along with our other two ranges, seemed like madness to me - unless I stopped making either the terracotta or black and white ranges, which I would never do.

I was talking at the time to Anthony Worrall Thompson, the celebrity chef and restaurateur. Anthony is a great fan of my Classic terracotta range and if I had been more organised we could have done great things together in England. We were sitting one day just shooting the breeze and maybe I complained that some shops were asking me to do coloured pottery and I didn't want to. (Melissa O'Neill, who ran Carrigaline Pottery for me, once said after a design meeting, "You're as bad as Terence Conran. Whatever brilliant ideas I come up with you both say 'Couldn't we just do it in white?!'" I said, "Sure why not Melissa? I bet you agree with me? Anyway, keep coming with your great ideas"). Anyway, I think it was Anthony who said, "You could always do blue. It's not really a colour and it always works with food. Years ago in China, it was the colour of the emperor's ware and has been used for thousands of years." I continued playing and realised that visually, blue doesn't fight with the food on the plate. I then came up with the cornflower idea. So as to maintain my purity of design, I put the blue cornflower in the centre of the plate and bowl so that as you start a meal you are eating from a white plate or bowl, which simply shows off the food with a fine blue line around the rim. Then, as you finish eating, the flower is there as a surprise. As a child I had a handmade porridge bowl made by my father's teacher Harry Davis. If I finished my porridge I got to see the tractor. I tried putting the cornflower into cups, but it would have driven our decorators mad and so it ended up outside the mugs for all to see.

All of this was twenty years ahead of its time and so apart from myself and a select few, nobody else really liked it (though Sinead Cusack and Jeremy Irons kitted out their new house completely with it). A few far-seeing people bought some, but then I stopped producing it. However in 2012, twenty-five years later, I re-launched it due to popular demand. Whenever I have a new idea or create a new design it always starts off slowly. I spend a lot of time working on the shape. For me design is not just an idea; it is the refinement of the idea that takes the time, and so when I put a new shape out to sell, it is usually so simple and unsensational that you could easily miss the fact that it's new and special. In fact, maybe I should have a special table for new pieces just to introduce them to you. Because of this subtlety though only a few of the new pieces sell at first. Then you go to dinner with a friend and you see the piece and think, "I didn't know that Stephen made this type of piece. It works really well, I must get one." Five years later and the piece is a winner.

I don't do sensational design. I'm like the old line in the marriage ceremony: I want to be the 'olive branch in the recess of your home', quietly there and loved. In the 1980s I made three sizes of what we now call 'decorated bowls' – generous serving bowls with a slightly Japanese curved silhouette and individually glazed rims. I made about twenty of each size that spring. By December, not one had sold and so I gave them away as Christmas presents. Three years later, I made a few more because I really liked them. They quickly became one of our best selling pieces and still are nearly thirty years later. When I design something new and nobody wants it, yes I feel a bit shitty and I do notice the old ego wobbling on its pedestal. Then I think, do I really believe in it? And if I do, I wait patiently until its time arrives and the idea returns to knock at my brain. S&P

BUILDING BLOCKS

"Good designers borrow,
great designers steal."
Steve Jobs

Angela Lansbury had been a good friend of my mother's and is in many ways very like her, both of them being strong, determined ladies with clear intelligence. I got to know Angela, her husband Peter Shaw and their whole family when they had a house in Conna in Co. Waterford. The success of her TV series *Murder She Wrote* however, meant that the family had to base themselves back in Hollywood where their son, Anthony, joined the family team in producing the series. The whole production was very much a family affair and their daughter, Deirdre, married an Italian and opened a wonderful restaurant in California.

Angela and Peter had been searching for a house in our area in the late 1980s. Finally, after two years of looking, they gave up on finding a house to buy and instead chose an amazing piece of land high on the cliffs looking out over the sea. Angela asked me would I design and build the house for her. As I have already mentioned, pottery is what I do but I have a real passion for designing and building houses; it's my hobby. I have always promised myself that I would never design a house for anyone except myself as I have very strong views on design and am also very precious about my ideas. In a way, design is what my whole life is about. I'm not saying that my designs are right, but they are me, for better or worse.

As we started designing the house I began to find out what I had already guessed, which was that it was an 'Angela and Peter house' with a Stevie P feel to it. Fortunately, both Angela and Peter were also very clear about what they wanted and had many brilliant ideas. They wanted my feel to

Interior and exterior details from Angela's house.

it, you know the anthem at this stage: wavy white walls, large Spanish tiles, lots of light coming from the south, (which in this case was even more sparkling coming from the open sea) and lots of plain wood. It needed to look like a set of old Irish farm buildings so that it would sit gently and naturally into the beautiful landscape. Angela got wonderful sumptuous sofas made and brought huge, white, handmade carpets that added to the feeling of comfort and space.

For more than a year, the faxes flew fast and furiously between the States and Ireland; it should be called 'the house designed by fax'. Angela would be in a rehearsal and would send over a sketch of some detail. Peter would get out of the shower and realise something that was important about bathrooms. Sometimes the carpenters would come, only to be told to stop as what they were doing right then had to be demolished. So progress would stop on that part of the house while it was decided whether the observation justified demolishing a wall or not. Thankfully I don't remember having to demolish anything.

One morning I went up to the site when the builders were putting on the wooden wall plates of the house from which the rafters would spring. They had decided to just put a metal strap over the wall plate and nail it to the wall. I made them take it all down and cement bolts into the wall for added strength. A year later a wind came in over the cliffs at over a 150 miles an hour. We

Above: Penn Castle, Shanagarry.
Below: Dave Murphy, Acting County Manager, aided and abbetted by Donal 'The Doc' O'Driscoll, turning the first sod for the Learning Centre.

have never had anything like that in east Cork. Whole farm sheds were blown away and caravans were literally picked up and blown out to sea. I was too frightened to go and see Angela's roof myself. I have a very vivid imagination, which goes against me at times. During the morning of the storm word got back to me that my bolts had held tight. Phew!

It was a great, energising project and when the house was finished Angela very generously gave me the money in 1990 to buy Shanagarry Castle, the former family home of William Penn. This was the perfect place for me to realise another dream: to create an international Learning Centre where I could build on my mother's passion for developing human intelligence.

I had known the castle since early childhood. The stream that passed beside it wandered easily through the rushes until it passed our house a quarter of a mile closer to the sea, and then on through the peat bog and bird sanctuary where Canada Geese and other migrating birds stop to rest and refuel on their long journeys. There are at least four types of wild duck, pheasant, pigeons, snipe, herons and many other birds. On the ground there are the odd otter, fox, hare, badger and a multitude of rabbits. When we were young, Simon and I would build boats and sail up to the castle where Sonny Daly lived with his mother. We were terrified of Sonny's mother as she was a wild looking woman living in very basic conditions. I'm sure as rumbustious young fellas we disturbed her peace and may have robbed her apples. Sonny was a lovely man. He would go

up to the pub for an occasional liquid refreshment then go back and sleep on a bale of hay. After his mother died the castle really didn't appear lived in. I had always had a great attachment to the castle and its location. It was like a piece of the world that time had forgotten. Built and added to from the 15th century over a five hundred year span, very little now remains except for part of a wall from the 1400s and a pretty much intact Victorian mock Gothic house with an unstable roof. For me though it's not the castle but the location that holds all its magic.

The castle has a long history. Of note are its connections with William Penn and the story told by a local priest that the Catholic Church was built right beside the castle while the owner was away. To hide the building work, the locals built high ricks of straw all around the construction work, hiding the new church from view until it was built.

William Penn Senior was possibly the best admiral that the British Navy ever had. He was a master tactician and his ideas were practiced by Raleigh, Nelson and even right up until the First World War. During the English Civil Wars in the 17th century, the English Crown was rotating between Protestant and Catholic monarchs. William Penn Senior was operating mainly in the Mediterranean off North Africa, Spain and Malta. At one point, there was no money to pay Penn and so he was given Macroom Castle in county Cork which also came with a huge amount of land. The Crown changed religion and Macroom with its fine land was taken

Above: With Patrick Scott hanging his first retrospective at the Douglas Hyde Gallery, Trinity College, Dublin.

Below: Angela and Lucy at a Christmas party.

back and in its stead he was given Shanagarry. Shanagarry was a cow shed in comparison to Macroom Castle. William Penn Junior was a bit of a tearaway and so to keep him out of trouble his father sent him to Shanagarry to manage his affairs. William Junior, being an intelligent young fellow, fell in with a group of Quakers in Cork City. As Quaker thinking was outside the vision of the Crown, Penn kept ending up in gaol in Cork and the father had to keep bailing him out. Eventually, the Queen and Penn Senior had enough and decided to give William Junior a piece of America called Sylvannia. On the boat to America, young William renamed his estate 'Pennsylvannia'. Penn, I suppose due to his Quaker convictions, was one of the very few settlers to negotiate with the Native Americans rather than killing them. It was possibly due to Penn's open, Quaker, liberal thinking that I had felt it would be appropriate to have the Learning Centre I had been yearning to do, in his castle.

My mother was an educator and a doctor in education and I have inherited her vision - though I think it's my daughter Lucy from my first marriage who will pull it all together. She has just self-published her first couple of books on essential topics for women and mothers and is fast becoming recognised as an important and clear thinker on mothering, creativity and women's empowerment.

Having been passionate about making pottery, building houses and creating employment, and when I have time left over from being passionate about the woman in my life, I am also passionate about real education. Looking with my eyes and thinking with my brain I constantly ask why things are the way they are and wonder if there might be a better way of doing things. Everything: politics, medicine, education, bringing decision-making to every community, world money, world food. At school I was rarely engaged by anything. Ask anyone who has done anything special with their lives and they will probably tell you that they were bored out of their minds in school. As an optimist, I assumed that within a couple of years of finishing school in 1962, the teachers and people who would have been through the same torture as me would see the light and change what is a teaching experience into a 'learning' experience. Every child to my mind has special talents. If Christians practised what they preach and 'God made man in His own image', then to me that means we are the same as God, we are God. God doesn't need to be taught anything, but that godliness needs to be nurtured and teased out of us. For a parent or anyone to think that they have the right to teach a child anything is absurd. The child knows all of the important stuff, they just need to be supported in learning to express their genius. Of course, there are things like sharp knives and hot fires. What I am talking about is the adult assumption that we adults are smart and kids need to be controlled and taught. I'm not saying that we don't need to teach brain surgeons their trade. I'm saying we must stop stifling natural intelligence in the first twenty years. Schools are mainly for teachers not for children. We are living in a world of largely unexploited potential because essentially there is almost no real education. The Oxford Dictionary's definition of the root of the word educate, *educare*, means 'to draw out that which is within.' Instead the system we cling to insists on stuffing in ideas and theories, which are mostly either untrue or out of date. I'm sure governments think education has moved forward over the past fifty years. It hasn't. There is now a thin veneer of inclusion, but children are still not respected by parents, Church or State. Name ten things you learned at school that have been of value to you then decide was it worth more than ten years of your life to learn them. My mother's definition of intelligence is not a college degree, but being able to see clearly what is right in front of your nose and having the courage to look. This idea is what I grew up with and I have always taken this with me.

Here is my confession. Knowing all of this I still sent my three children to school; they all came out of it the worse for wear. I was so into what I was doing that I didn't take twelve years out of my life to do road trips and build tree houses, rear animals and grow trees and flowers and visit people doing interesting as well as not so interesting things (although thankfully Lauren did). When I regard it as so important why didn't I do it? Well I didn't, to my eternal shame, but I did have a dream for Shanagarry.

The village of Shanagarry never had what I would call a centre, what in Italy is a piazza or town square where people and children naturally and informally meet up with each other. I reckoned that by developing Shanagarry Castle, adding what I called the Gallery on the side and creating a formal garden with rills of running water like the Alhambra in Granada, that all this combined with our beautiful beach would be a wonderful place to explore and draw out that magical essence that we all have. It is my contention that our lives are as big or as small as our thinking. There is nothing wrong in having a small life, but it is important that the dreamers should have room to dream and not be under the constraints of society to conform to a pre-ordained pattern. And furthermore, a pattern which wasn't created to assist and support them but to control them. In

fact, it is a pattern created to limit and control the natural, joyous expression of creation of which we are all children with unique talents and potential. I was lucky to have a mother who really got this and so I will be a natural playful child until the day I die, and then some.

Given this paradise of Shanagarry (which from Gaelic means 'Old Garden'), through the castle and my imagination I started to create a real heaven on earth – a place where people would want to come and explore possibilities that they had sometimes dreamed of, or maybe not even dreamed of, until they arrived. With an inspirational space, gardens, a gallery, great food, a bar and a working Pottery downstairs to create a vibrant energy, I believed great things would happen. The Pottery was the anchor and it meant that there would be money coming in to subsidise the Learning Centre. I envisioned benches outside the front door where people could sit and chat on warm evenings. There would be employment for about fifty people, and while I didn't know how it would develop, I had at least three target groups that I knew would enjoy and respond to the activities and atmosphere.

The first group I had in mind for the Learning Centre was for people aged sixteen to twenty-six who might be unclear as to where they were going or couldn't buy into the values offered by mainline education (bearing in mind that east Cork has one of the highest suicide rates for young men in this age group in Europe). The second group was those aged between forty and fifty-five. Young people are not trained for life. They are told to specialise at a very early age for a particular career so that by the middle of their working life, if they lose their job, it is often very hard to adjust and explore new possibilities. My third group was the over-60s. Many people reach retirement age without having found their calling in life. Now that they are free from the nine-to-five job, they have time to look, wonder and explore on the foundation of a lifetime of experience. All of these three groups have an enormous potential for themselves and for society, but where do they start? There is no government programme or EU directive that can create this magic. It needs inspired and dedicated people.

It was a great dream and an important dream. Although we can all dream, we need a few visionaries without boundaries around to make sure the world doesn't fall into a silent, unhappy sleep. People like Mahatma Gandhi, Martin Luther King Jr, and Nelson Mandela really got this. Unfortunately, some of the great modern day-dreamers, whilst realising that it only takes one person to change the world, forgot that with dreaming goes love and responsibility for the people around you. I am thinking of people like Stalin, Mao Tse-tung and Hitler. All of these men understood that any one person is capable of changing the future direction of their country.

Shanagarry Castle was a romantic name for some ruins. I was in love with it because of its south facing aspect and its potential. By building the Gallery and Pottery Workshop on one side I was able to enclose what was a formal garden with old-fashioned fruit trees, a rose arbour and the most complete collection of original Chinese roses outside of China, courtesy of my good friend Roger Phillips. There was to be an orangery filled with old varieties of lemon and orange trees and a medieval medicinal herb garden. Lauren designed and planted the gardens along with Roger, who found beautiful rare and native plants to fill and expand her plans considerably. Details such as rills (small channels of running water) and comprehensive collections of water irises, old varieties of apples and a general sense of quirky antiquity were added. Roger planned a marsh walk and designed mosaic benches made using my pottery, to be placed at restful spots in the garden. Though she won't let me say it, the garden was Lauren's dream and it was she who executed it with Roger's inspiration, support and knowledge of suppliers.

Whenever money ran low over the years I would go to Paul McGowan and ask where I might find some. One such occasion was the Castle Project. I think I have always slightly surprised Paul by the scope of my schemes and how often I have succeeded. He has never wavered in his support, without which much that I have done would never have happened. I remember putting the Castle Project to Paul in his office. He looked at me and said, "I suppose you want to know how to raise the money?" I replied, "Yes." He looked at me like a judge passing a sentence and said, "I suppose you are ready for the Business Expansion Scheme?" He was flattering me. BES had very strict rules and was carefully monitored. That Paul felt I was up to BES despite my wild nature felt really empowering to me.

So the money was coming in and building work was flying. Someone in County Hall suggested that a very modern addition might solve an integrity issue with one of the joining parts of the castle which had fallen down long ago. Given that the castle already had sections built at four different times through the centuries, we felt it would be a great idea to add something from our own time. I wanted something very pure and clear with simple lines and so I brought someone over from Norman Foster's office in London to throw some ideas at me. Lauren was planning a vast wall of mirrored glass which would reflect the gardens and front the Learning Centre with its modern equipment and computers for research. We were seventy percent of the way there when unfortunately the Doc had to retire due to ill health. Dave Murphy also retired around this time. I could have handled the project myself as I knew that Dave and the Doc were there to bounce ideas off. However, disaster then struck in a way that changed my career and life forever. Suffice to say that due to differences of opinion between the newly appointed Bishop of Cobh and myself the project ground to a halt and the Learning Centre could never be realised.

For myself and for mankind I have always wanted the most human kindness possible for everyone. I see life as simple. We do something we enjoy. We eat. We sleep calmly and we care for everyone and the planet. It's not difficult and yet when I see the people who run the world, bankers, politicians and religious leaders, it appears that they are all so greedy that the human race is merely a means to their own ends. It is March 2013 and the Syrian people are being massacred while the world stands idly by. A survey has just shown that fifty percent of food produced for human consumption is thrown away. Ever since I was a child, the lack of common sense and caring for humankind has staggered me. Just look around. The list is endless. We live in heaven but allow it to be hell. Do we have no imagination? Because it is us, individually, who allow this cruel madness. Enough said. I just wanted to give you a sense of why I am so angry, sad and disappointed that I was unable to create a new perspective through my projected Learning Centre. I still care deeply and try not to pollute my life with anger. I can really feel the frustration and sense of powerlessness that the tens of millions of totally unnecessary refugees on my planet experience.

I am not one to be constrained and so despite all of this I drove forward with my other plans. It was a rollercoaster of a time, a time of great celebration and sadness. My son Oran was born in the summer of 1993 and my father died that autumn. We were producing three full ranges of pottery: my Classic terracotta, Celebration and now Shanagarry, which Philip had just left me. We desperately needed more space and so I planned the new building beside Shanagarry Castle. White and airy with lots of natural light, it would house my new Pottery and a Gallery. Creating a new flowing workspace on the ground floor for producing Shanagarry pottery was a high priority. The concept was to have a spacious, streamlined pottery on the ground floor with clay entering one end and moving forward until pots were packed for delivery going out the far end.

Upstairs was a huge empty area with a small restaurant at one end and a balcony overlooking the bird sanctuary and Ballycotton Bay. I applied my idea that a shop is like a movie set and constantly changing. With this in mind the space could be used for exhibitions, a shop or yoga and learning activities. From any of the large circular windows there were beautiful views across the bird sanctuary, Ballycotton Bay or out over the formal gardens. Pat Scott had the idea for generously proportioned arched openings downstairs, topped by the ocular windows inspired by a Ballymaloe farm building. The arches sprang from Kilkenny limestone corbels on which a few different sculptors came to work, creating individual carvings. For the paving outside I used local light coloured Cloyne limestone.

I opened the top floor of the Gallery in June 1993 with a Patrick Scott Retrospective exhibition of his work from 1943 right up to 1993. As Pat had been involved in the design of the building, we had made certain that there would be plenty of natural light for the exhibition. We held the show in the early summer which afforded additional light from the sun's reflection off the sea a hundred metres away. The space and the paintings were magic. Pat and Lauren spent days choosing and hanging the exhibition to the highest professional standards. Through all of his phases Pat's work has graced our walls and it always asks eternal questions. For me, art should ask questions, not answer them. I love the simplicity, the grace, timelessness and the uniqueness of each piece. This is reinforced for me by having spent a lot of time with him and having worked on many projects together. Most things with my name on them contain a lot of Pat's thoughts. Knowing him so well and having been to almost all of his exhibitions, I am always bowled over by his new work. It is fresh, exciting, relaxing and meditative, and though closely related, every piece is exquisitely unique. I can't imagine life without Pat. I intended spending at least an hour every day in the Gallery while the exhibition was on, just being there quietly with the paintings. And I needed all of the meditation I could get. There is no way to describe my sense of loss and entrapment when the Learning Centre was killed off. It was to be the culmination

of my expression of sharing my mother's wisdom. The emotional pain and anger were far greater than losing the whole Pottery some twelve years later.

Both before and after Pat's exhibition, Lauren had been travelling and visiting craft and design trade fairs in Paris, New York, London and Frankfurt. It was our plan that while we restored the old castle buildings we would use the gallery space as an emporium like the original ones in Hong Kong, spectacularly full of beautiful handmade goods, and of course our pottery and Simon's glass. Eventually, the shop would move to the old castle and the Gallery would once again be a gallery of Patrick Scott paintings with other activities going on at the same time.

We were determined that the Gallery was going to be the most amazing shop in Ireland, on a totally different level to my previous shops. And it was, thanks to Lauren's taste. My first shops with Jim were the best of Irish craft and design made in Ireland. For the Gallery, we wanted to stock items that we ourselves loved using and that were made with care from natural materials to a simple, timeless design, sourced from all over the world as well as Ireland. I am proud to have been part of it and am delighted that we did it. Okay, no accountant or banker would say that, but a world without creative madness is hell for me.

The interior and balcony café of the Emporium overlooking Ballycotton Bay 1995.

The Gallery was intended to be my last stand in shopkeeping, and so it had to be spectacular. It had a huge turf fire in the centre and sunlight poured in from the skylights to make everything sparkle naturally. There was lots of airy space to move around in. I had the most wonderful shelving made from evergreen oak that I had bought from the County Council when they were widening the road at Dunkettle near Cork. There were a couple of local limestone tables made from slabs rejected when a new extension was being built for Cork University, and on these we displayed the pottery, Simon's luminous glass and Ciaran Forbes stunning wooden bowls. I had three marble tables made especially in Italy and I imported a container of softly hued terracotta floor tiles from Spain. As always the Gallery was not about maximising sales: it was about giving people a great experience. I have always needed to find a business partner who will say, "Okay you create an amazing experience, now let me turn it into money."

My mind was moving very fast at the time I opened the Gallery. Originally I wanted everything to open together: Learning Centre, gardens, restaurant, Pottery, shop and gallery. Logistically though it wasn't happening, so I opened the Pottery downstairs, then Pat's exhibition in the Gallery upstairs, then the shop. S&P

GOLD

"To bring beauty into your life, that's my job."
Stephen Pearce

During this time of luxurious madness I was also dreaming up my porcelain and gold range. As a young potter, I was lucky enough to be taken by my father to visit an Austrian potter in London called Lucie Rie. I instantly loved her pots and became a great admirer of her work. Her shapes were very fine and thought out, as opposed to the simplicity of mine. She made quite tight, small pots mostly in matte white porcelain with a matte black manganese rim; they had great individuality. At the time, I was taking full advantage of the earthenware clay to make large loose pots. Since then I had promised myself I would spend my twilight years making fine sensitive pots in porcelain as Lucie Rie has done. I will put gold rims where she had used black manganese and they will have a very eastern feel.

Although 1995 was the busiest year of my life, I kept taking on new projects. Maybe I sensed the Bishop at my back door and like a plant in tough times that flowers and fruits like mad, I had to express myself in every way possible. I also wanted to celebrate all that had been achieved by the Pottery and so I rushed full tilt into the Gold range. In fact, in preparation for this I had already installed equipment for processing porcelain in the new Pottery building.

Philip Wood came over once again and recommended a porcelain clay and developed a glaze to fit. Now I need to tell you something about glaze. In pottery, developing a glaze to fit your clay is critical. Each and every clay has its own rate of expansion and contraction during heating and cooling. This happens to a greater degree when firing a glazed pot at about 1000°C in our kilns than in a domestic oven where the temperature is much lower. As the clay expands and contracts the glaze must move with the clay. If the glaze flows too much and is too big for the clay body, tensions are set up between the clay and the glaze, which means the pottery can become unpredictable when in use. As little tension as possible is best but there must be a slight tension. If the glaze is too small for the clay body it is like putting on a shirt that is too tight and rips at the seams. So when the glaze is just a fraction too small, little cracks form in it; this is called 'crazing'. In the East this is a highly prized and much admired effect. I once worked in a Pottery in Japan where we would take scalding hot pots out of the kiln and dip them straight into used car oil so that the crazing would go black. 'Antiquing' we called it!

Once Philip had got the glaze to fit our new porcelain clay perfectly, I then got him to change the recipe so that the glaze would be too small and so form crazing. For stoneware and porcelain one uses a lot of glaze materials that are natural and therefore variable. For example, while serving my first apprenticeship in England with Ray Finch, one of the most important ingredients for his glaze was ash from the household fire. To make the glaze more interesting chicken bones were burned in the fire. One week, for some reason, the chickens came from a different source - I think it was that they were from a supermarket rather than the local farmer - and believe it or not the glaze came out slightly different than normal.

More than a thousand years ago there was a potter in China who had been commissioned to make ware for the Emperor. He would have used ash from rice straw and from selected roots and trees according to recipes handed down over generations. Old-fashioned, wood-fired kilns such as I used in Japan had no instrumentation and so depended on spy holes around the chamber where one could see and monitor how the glaze was doing. Some clay rings, with glaze on them, could also be drawn out through these holes to assess the state of the glaze during the firing. I became very good at judging how kilns were progressing simply by looking in. I love looking into the white heat where everything appears to be dancing and yet the state of the glaze is pretty clear. Our Chinese potter was having a bad kiln day however, and ran out of options. He was at maximum temperature. If you go too hot when firing porcelain (a first cousin to glass) the pots begin to bend and collapse. To control the kiln one has the option of dropping the temperature slightly or holding it. It is also possible to reduce the amount of air going in to the fire-boxes. (This is called reduction and means that combustion is incomplete and carbon remains in the atmosphere of the kiln. It is this that can alter different glazes in different ways, affecting the colour and texture and giving interesting effects to the porcelain.) The Chinese potter tried everything he had ever learnt to control his kiln, but to no avail. It would not obey his wishes. Finally, in total despair, he jumped into the flames. When the kiln cooled, a brilliant red glaze was found on everything. The Emperor was delighted as no one had ever seen such a brilliant red before. It was called *sang de boeuf;* at least that is the folklore!

I had a similar experience while I was working with Gwyn Hanssen Piggott at a time when she was borrowing Michael Cardew's Pottery in Cornwall from him. Michael had designed and built a circular kiln that was the most temperamental beast of a kiln that I have ever had the misfortune to fire. (Gwyn could be strong willed enough at times too! She is still one of my very favourite potters.) We got the kiln heated up to a certain point but it wouldn't continue to rise in temperature as it should. For twenty-four hours it remained stuck at about 1200°C. There was complete disarray. Gwyn would feed the fireboxes and then send her minions around to put more wood in. Then she would go off in a huff of frustration. To fire

Closing down the kiln at Cardew Pottery in Cornwall while listening to "Little Red Rooster".

a difficult kiln, one person needs to be in charge. You live with it from start to finish. You talk to the kiln. You watch the chimney. You adjust the air and you know exactly what to do. You cannot fire a kiln by committee. Finally Gwyn called Richard Batterham, my good friend and favourite potter, who lived about two hours away. Richard arrived, took one look at the kiln and said you are choking it. We let the fires die down and eventually, as if by magic, the temperature started to rise and by gentle stoking we got to the correct temperature in another six hours. I have a photo of me standing on the roof of the shed covering the chimney, listening to Mick Jagger and his *Little Red Rooster*. I am no longer sure exactly what year that was but I remember vividly standing on that roof and trying to balance while hallucinating with exhaustion waiting for the heat to rise and feeling the shots of Keith Richards' guitar shooting through me.

In some ways earthenware is much simpler but also more difficult. In both porcelain and stoneware the clay body fuses into a glass-like material because of the high temperature and nature of the clay. Stoneware fires to around 1280°C and porcelain at 1300°C to 1320°C. With earthenware we fire to 1100°C and it always remains porous and, somewhat like timber, continues to move a bit all of its life, which is what makes it so interesting to me. Therefore, getting an earthenware glaze that fits is nigh impossible. In time, earthenware almost always crazes. I know I am biased but I love earthenware; I find it more sympathetic to touch and hold (like a good wife).

Now, back to my new gold porcelain range. With the technical side just right – thanks in most part to Philip Wood for all the glaze tests and for finding a strange man in Manchester who sold us gold at £50 a drop – I was now ready to launch one of my life's ambitions: small porcelain pots with gold rims and a light glaze to complement the colour of the clay. I started on it myself and soon realised that it was never going to

Angela Treacy creating the gold porcelain range.

happen. I had so many major projects on the go I was literally flying in all directions.

I had always liked the pots of one of our top potters, Angela Treacy, who had been making pottery with me for a good twenty years. Angela has a great sensitivity and feel for the clay and gets exactly what I am about. I felt that together we could create a great range. I had originally seen her becoming the queen of the blue range. When that didn't work out, I had the idea that she could become the princess of the gold and crackle. Immediately when she started I was amazed. Angela got exactly what I was on about and really got the Eastern thing completely. She understood what I wanted, even when I didn't. It was one of the most satisfying times for me as a potter. It was a long course of trial and error that we followed. I had a strong direction in my head, but often between taking something from my head and making a three-dimensional object of it, the realisation of the idea was not what I thought it would be. I think marriage is like that too. You find someone whom you adore more each day then, either suddenly or slowly, you realise that the person is not who you thought they were. Of course, they have always just been themselves but your mind had built up expectations around them that they could never fulfil.

The progress of Angela and I developing the Gold range was like that. I had a clear image in my mind of the shapes. I would explain to Angela and she would make what she thought I wanted and it would be different. Sometimes it was her interpretation and sometimes what I really wanted was different to what I explained to her. Fortunately we had worked together long enough for us both to realise it was just a process. Slowly the shapes evolved, frequently the glazing changed too and then the shapes had to change to work with the new ideas of where the glaze and gold rim were going. My only regret is that because there was so much going on at the time, I couldn't spend more time with Angela. I love all of the different pieces that we make at Shanagarry, but Angela's gold will always hold a special place in my heart.

We launched the Gold range with all of the usual fanfare and it fell on its face flat as a pancake. Again we were thirty years ahead of our time and, in the end, we sold it all off as seconds. I will never forgive myself for not packing away a couple of pieces of each shape.

Apart from Patrick Scott's paintings, I try very hard not to become attached to objects and yet I still feel I am knee deep and drowning in things I have collected over the years. The Japanese had it right. They lived in paper and wood houses. Of course the risk of fire was enormous, if not from their own houses then maybe from one of the houses next door. One of the ways of dealing with this was to keep a lot of their money invested in special pottery. For centuries important people in Japan kept a large part of their wealth in valuable pottery so that if your house went on fire and you could get out with ten pots it was the equivalent of a million euros. Lesser merchants might escape the blaze with fifty to two hundred thousand euros worth. When potters like Kaneshige, in each of the six main pottery areas, were made a Living National Treasure, it meant that if you bought a pot from them it often had a name. It was presented in an individually handmade box signed by the master. When we unloaded Kaneshige's kiln and he chose the pieces, a local box maker would arrive on his bicycle to measure each pot and make a box for it. A couple of weeks later when we had wrapped each pot in a top quality piece of silk and put it in its box, company directors would start to arrive, one per day, in chauffeur driven limos. Sometimes Kaneshige would make them wait kneeling on the cobblestones in his porch for hours. Then they would be led by the daughter-in-law into a fair-sized room with a small table in the middle. They would kneel at the table and after a while Kaneshige would come and sit at the opposite side of the table. Kaneshige's wife would then start to slowly bring in a series of pots one by one. She would choose some great pots and some crap ones. At each pot, learned discussions would take place with ooohing and aaahing and grunts and snorts would ensue. From the noises, Kaneshige's wife who would be waiting discretely outside the door would know if the customer actually knew anything about pottery or not. Once she knew, she would serve top quality green tea after the fashion of the Tea Ceremony. Then she would bring in a pot all wrapped up and ready to go. A cheque for between €10,000 and a €50,000 changed hands discretely and the man would go out to his car often not knowing what the wife had given him for his money. Of course Kaneshige couldn't fool people all of the time. However, anything you bought from him was guaranteed to go up in value faster than the stock exchange. **S⚜P**

PUBS, PLAYSCHOOL & CREATIVE FLOURISHING

"You either die of boredom or exhaustion."
Anon

In 1995, at the same time as launching the Gold Range, I was buying a pub in Ballycotton and restoring it in readiness for the making of the film *Divine Rapture* with Marlon Brando, Johnny Depp, Debra Winger and John Hurt. I was also opening a playschool for our youngest daughter, Mirin, in Kilmahon, my father's old house, as well as buying Carrigaline Pottery from two Brazilians living in Brazil. Heady times! The playschool took priority. Creating our own educations seems to run in the family. My mother had been an early collaborator with Maria Montessori and although they disagreed on some things they were both similar in that they refused to be treated as second-class citizens just because they were women. They both saw the road to freedom as being through education and were amongst the first women in Europe to seriously challenge men in their ivory towers. I am grateful for what rubbed off on me as well as on my children. As my mother used to say, "Intelligence is being able to see what is right in front of your nose. What we need is always there."

Ann O'Riordan, an energetic and inspired playschool teacher from Ballycotton, came to start the playschool with about a dozen children at the beginning. Ann had the necessary quality for leading a group. She really loves children, collectively and individually. Maria Montessori and my mother would have been very happy to see the start those children got. I wanted Mirin to have fun and meet other kids and I wanted to provide a safe, creative and supportive place that the children of the Pottery employees could spend time in. I also wanted to carry on my mother's tradition of making equipment available so that Mirin and the other children could begin their road to finding out what they liked and who they were, using and creating for themselves toys made out of natural materials.

While the playschool made sense, the pub was a moment of madness. As most of the bars in Ireland became modernised (except for their toilets) I yearned for a pub where I could enjoy a pint in old-fashioned surroundings without a television, with a non-smoking room and men and women's loos that were clean. I found a bar in nearby Ballycotton which hadn't been modernised through the 1970s phase of beauty-boards. In cleaning up the bar, I left all of the original detail. There was a small coal fire, which was always lit in the winter and always smoked. The old woodwork I painted in a traditional cream and light brown with wood grain feathered on it. John Beausang, who came to run the bar for me, put fresh sawdust on the worn, red floor tiles every evening and made sure there were candles flickering on the tables. It was always a real pleasure to walk in to. We restored an old inner courtyard and put a piano in the back room that people would occasionally be moved to play.

Once, Thomas Kenneally (who had written *Schindler's List*) was visiting Ireland writing some articles about his trip. My pub was one of the locations chosen. As production of *Divine Rapture* had just come to a premature demise due to financial difficulties, I quickly got Michael Sheedy, our local monumental mason to do me an old-fashioned gravestone, which read 'Divine Rapture, Born 10 July 1995, Died 23 July 1995'. When I arrived at the pub for the interview, the stone was just being set in cement by the door. I saw it as a local landmark. Unfortunately, some neighbours didn't agree with me, so I took it up. However, it still made the front page of the Hollywood Gazette, not to mention the front page of the local paper and TV news. Eventually though I sold the pub, largely because I was getting too fond of the drink and it was a distraction from the rest of my life.

In the early 1930s Carrigaline Pottery was in its infancy. The Keeling family came over from England at the invitation of Hodder Roberts in 1928. Louis Keeling invited my father to design pottery for him in 1938, but my father said he knew nothing about pottery, which was true at the time. When I was a child we always kept milk and lemonade (this was before the days of fridges) in wonderful half-gallon Carrigaline jugs which were of a friendly, simple shape with plain terracotta on the outside. Then there were the well-known blue and cream horizontal bands, beloved by many. Because I knew Louis' son Alan who ran Carrigaline for years, and because I knew the Gays of Carrigaline who were also involved, I followed their Pottery's difficult history. For many years, Carrigaline Pottery grew steadily from its modest beginnings and became an industrial factory with almost everything made by machine. At the same time there was a lot of skilled handwork, such as that involved in making the pieces of a teapot and assembling them, hand decorating and banding and a lot more. At one point in its history Carrigaline was even producing tiles. When I heard that it was about to close I went into negotiations with the Brazilians who owned it. I was full of energy at the time. I felt nostalgia for the place and the employees, and furthermore I believed that, with tight local management and a close focus on product range, it could be turned around. There was a great skilled and wonderful workforce, for which it must have been heartbreaking to have one disaster follow another in management terms, and I will always admire them for rolling up their sleeves yet again when I arrived.

My vision for Carrigaline was that as it was big enough to make reasonably large runs of ware, it was also small enough to do relatively short runs cost effectively. I felt that there was a bright future ahead. Unfortunately, a large loan that I thought had been written off by the bank in order to allow the company to survive suddenly reared its ugly head. Someone decided "sure Pearce has plenty of money." I knew nothing about running a pottery factory this size. Interestingly, at that time both Carrigaline and our own Pottery were employing about 90 people each. We were a large handcraft Pottery and

Carrigaline was a small industrial Pottery. Each one had completely different production methods requiring very different skills. I was aware of this at the time and so I hired an Englishman with a strong background in the pottery business from Stoke-on-Trent, where pottery on this scale originated and where, before they all started amalgamating into Wedgwood, Denby et al., there were literally dozens of Carrigaline type Potteries.

Melissa O'Neill, a close friend of Lauren's from her university days, had been a buyer for Terence Conran's Heals (the modern furniture and home furnishing store) in London. I admired her eye for design and how she made her choices. I thought that if Melissa could set a course for the company design-wise, then surely between the rest of us we could figure out how to manufacture it? Unfortunately, with me only touching the ground in places with the large amount of projects I was juggling, I missed a lot of what was going on and finally Melissa resigned. I still have tremendous admiration for Melissa and would do it all again, only this time the brief would be different and she would be only playing to her strengths with proper sup-

Various Carrigaline ranges, with Darina and I happily designing a range specially for her. However 9/11 killed Carrigaline before we had time to produce the designs.

port and me on the case. I'm not quite perfect but I am working on it. About six more lifetimes and I'll be a different man. Maybe!

With Carrigaline, I never managed to put a clear strategy in place and it muddled along losing money for six years. Then finally a profitable year arrived, despite the fact that I had never managed to implement my vision. We had secured contracts for something like twenty-two new hotels which were to open in the following twelve months and, thanks to Bewley's and Musgraves, the company had turned around. Then bang: 9/11. Almost none of the new Irish hotels opened. The existing hotels and restaurants were buying as little as possible and the big English companies started dumping pottery on the Irish market as they had the same problem as us but on a much larger scale. Before 9/11 the wholesale price of a Carrigaline-made industrial mug was just under a euro; it was hard, but we could manage it so long as we were selling some more profitable items with it. Suddenly, a mug was thirty cent and less. We just couldn't live with that. So bang for us. Luckily, the site of the factory was being watched by two supermarkets so we just about came out clean from the whole affair. What lessons did I learn? None, so I kept on expanding.

One of the heroes of my own Pottery was Fumio Otsuka. I received a phone call from CTT (now the Enterprise Board) one day

Trying to look serious and Japanese beside Fumio. I think I succeed. Opposite: Trying and failing to find a space to be creative in.

in 1990 saying that they were bringing a high-powered Sony executive to Cork and could they come visit us as they knew I spoke Japanese and had a feel for the culture. I said sure, and I will prepare lunch. When the boys from CTT saw the sushi they suddenly had something important to do in Cork. Fumio and I got stuck in and got on well. We later headed to the pub and he stayed the night. Fumio explained that the Japanese trade board got together top Japanese companies to lend middle management people like him to them. They were then sent to foreign countries like Ireland to help us export to Japan. He offered to help me do this. I said to him, "Fumio, I know you guys. You are here to get inside our computers, to extract information to help Toyota and the rest to sell into Ireland." "Oh!" he said, "in that case can we be friends?" "Sure" I replied. He came to visit me a few more times during his stay and then went back to Japan. At this stage the Pottery was expanding again and I was thinking of diversifying into other things like making linens and glass and different product ranges, as well as more shops. We seemed unstoppable. I began to wonder if we were ok. Was I smart? Was there something I was missing? Should I be setting up management structures? Should I slow down? I had a brain wave: Fumio had the unique experience of having worked for almost fifty years with the two founders of Sony, Ibuka the inventor and physicist, and the sales genius, Morita. Fumio himself had risen to Vice President of sales and had been involved with a Sony joint venture in making golf clubs. So before he left Ireland, I called him and said, "If you ever feel like coming back to Ireland and working for me and playing a little golf, here is my number." Two years later, I got a fax from Fumio saying, "I am ready to come and work for you, do you want me?" I replied immediately and wrote, "Of course I want you. How much should I pay you?" "Make me an offer and I will accept it," he answered. I went into Midleton, our local town, and asked a bank manager how much he was earning and he told me £30,000. I promptly faxed Fumio saying, "I will pay you £30,000." to which he

replied, "I accept. Will you pay for my ticket over?" Of course, I said, and so he came. Sony Dublin sent down a van load of samples, several Sony TVs, Sony PCs and video players and a pile of other bits and pieces. It was like Christmas. Fumio asked me what did I want him to do. I said look at everything in the company and tell me if there is something that I am missing. Then tell me how you would run the company and why. Then teach us all about sales. Off he went into his little corner and tap, tap, tap on the laptop, rooting through files, with questions for everyone. Finally, we sat down and I said, "So?" He said, "Ahso, very interesting. I can find no problem. Your company is text book example for company this size. As you grow we must put in checks and controls." Fumio always wanted to take the Pottery to the stock market. He said he could raise me fifteen times the value of the company. I just didn't want to lose control. In hindsight, it would have been great because I wouldn't have been able to do some of the stupid things that I did, but I've no regrets. I am a free man, a bit in debt but we'll handle that too, all in good time.

Despite everything that was going on in the mid-1990s and apart from the fact that I had been flat out on multiple projects for ten years, I couldn't get any peace to just let ideas drop in to my mind. There were meetings, meetings, meetings and banks that were treating me well, but there was a lot of it. Planning permits, bureaucracy, growing the Pottery, I was busy but not doing what I enjoyed doing. I kept finding peaceful corners to put my potter's wheel in so that I could let my inspiration flow and be creative. It would gather dust. I'd find another corner away from phones and radios. The joke was, where will we move your wheel next? I am an ideas man; keep me away from paperwork if you want to get any value from me. I knew I had to get out if I wanted to stay sane. In fact, the only thing that kept me sane was talking to Lauren. She is a great listener and very supportive and just the shoulder I needed to lean on.

By the mid-1990s though I was getting more and more stressed and I had two little children fast growing up that I was too busy to spend much time with. Finally Lauren said to me, "Stephen, you can spend the next five years becoming more stressed, getting another ulcer, or we can move out for a couple of years. We could do what we have always said we'd like to and give Mirin and Oran the opportunity to experience living

in another country with a different culture to absorb." She pointed out that it would also give me a chance to catch my breath and go back to doing what I love most: being creative. We had often discussed this, believing that one of the best educational experiences we could give our children was a sense of ease living amidst other cultures and learning a couple of languages so that in the future they could move around the world with confidence. Lauren did eventually take me off to Italy and later to France. The children learned to speak Italian and French and with a little more peace in my life I started painting and sculpting.

Lauren and I were married in Florence. I had suggested Rome as a joke as lots of Irish Catholics go to Rome to get married so that they can have a quiet wedding. It seemed like a good idea for two non-Christians to go to Rome to be married in the town hall there. However Lauren, ever the art historian, knew the town hall in the Palazzo Signoria in Florence was more romantic, although the first question in the Italian wedding ceremony was, "Do you wish to share your assets forever or keep them separate?" There is a separate ceremony for each possibility, a far cry from 'the olive branch in the recess of the home'!

The next year, we finally decided to move to Italy for a year so that we could be at peace together as a family and so that I could finally get on with designing again away from the stresses that were wearing me down. Our plan was one year in Italy, one year in France, then Thailand and South America. However, Lauren thought that because Mirin and Oran had done such a good job learning Italian that they should be rewarded with a year of not having to learn a new language and to just enjoy being with their new Italian friends. So we stayed a second year and I immersed myself in painting, making bronze sculptures and working with Italian craftsmen making new pottery designs for the shops, which were constantly clamouring for something new every season.

Apart from Japan, I had never come across a country like Italy where craftspeople take their work so seriously. I prefer the Italian ethic to the Japanese though. Top Japanese craftspeople are amazing but they take themselves very seriously and are often only interested in themselves and how wonderful they are. The Italians on the other hand are the real deal. They have incredible skill and patience combined with adaptability and a willingness to think outside the box to create a solution to something new. I would go to welding shops

and just observe. I love watching skilled crafts people at work. Eventually, after a few years, I became known as "*il grande artiste*" partly in jest because I am so tall. The emphasis was on *grande* but also because I always think outside the box and say, "What if?" Florence is the exception where they seem a bit stuck in the past except for a few exciting young designers like Massimo Bianchi who designed Lauren's unusual eternity ring hand-carved from a piece of ebony.

At first I found the food and wine very hard to take and it wasn't very long before I went on strike against pasta, whereas today Mirin and Oran still love it and have no interest in spuds at all. Over time, I warmed to Italian food and I now love to cook and eat it. My three favourite foods are Vietnamese, Italian and Japanese in that order. Ireland and Italy for me have an equal number of similarities and dissimilarities. So many things in Italy go back centuries in a long steady line. In Ireland, probably because of having been colonised for so long and then because of the Famine, we really had the stuffing knocked out of us in so many ways, and yet we are still here.

Around this time, when I was beginning to feel uncomfortable in the Pottery, I started sitting at the kitchen table with a collection of water colours. At first I only allowed myself yellow, red and blue. I tried to let go of ideas and just let feelings come out. As soon as it began to flow after several

Above: Trying to look imperial, which for some reason Lauren, Don and Martha all find amusing, leaving the bar post wedding.

Below: My impression of the Pyrennees.

Relaxing before an opening.

*Opposite: Wandering
on Mt. Fuji in France.*

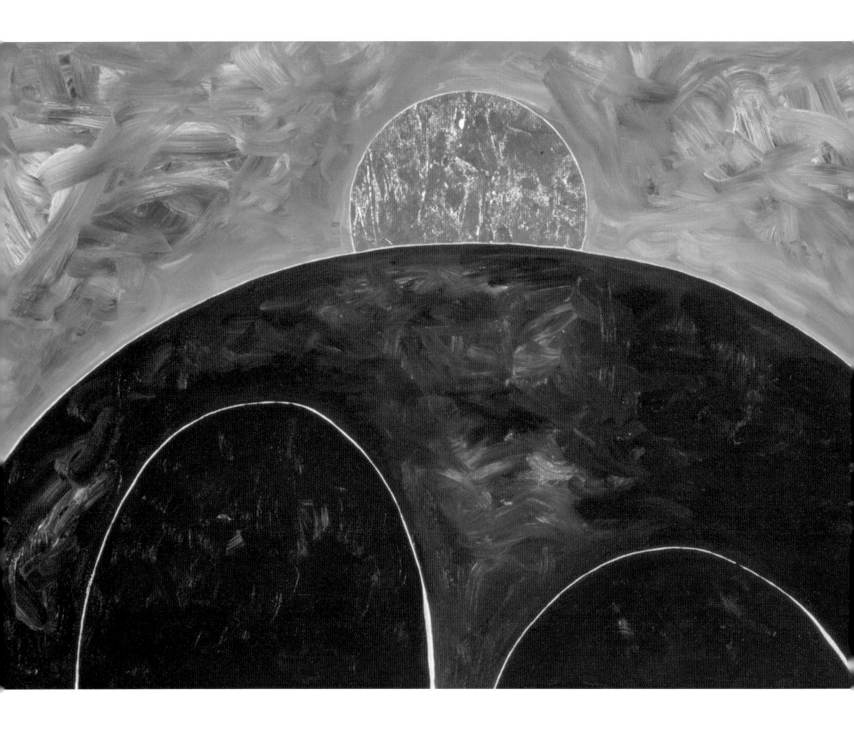

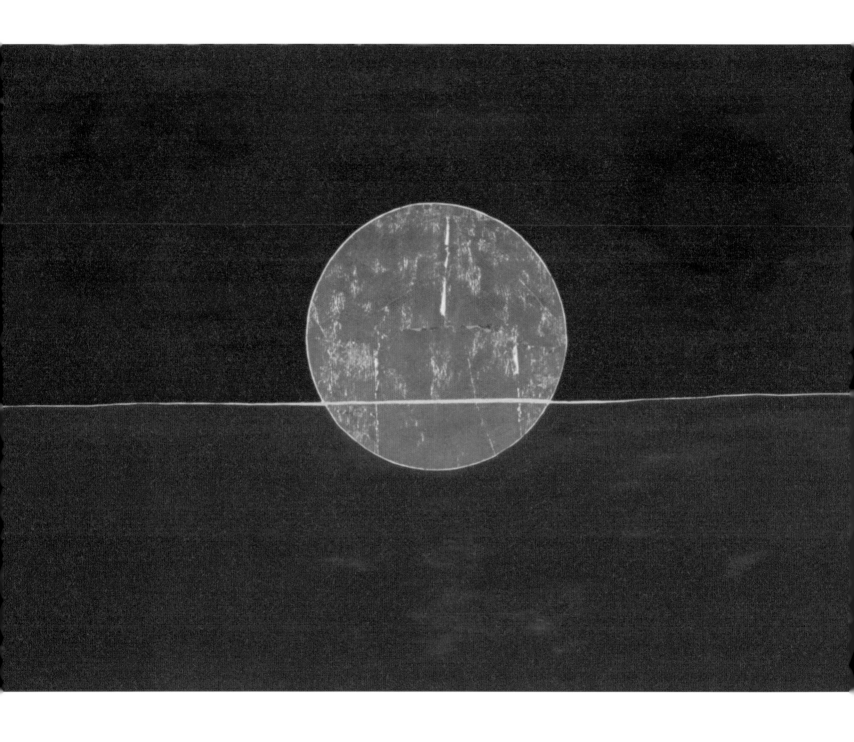

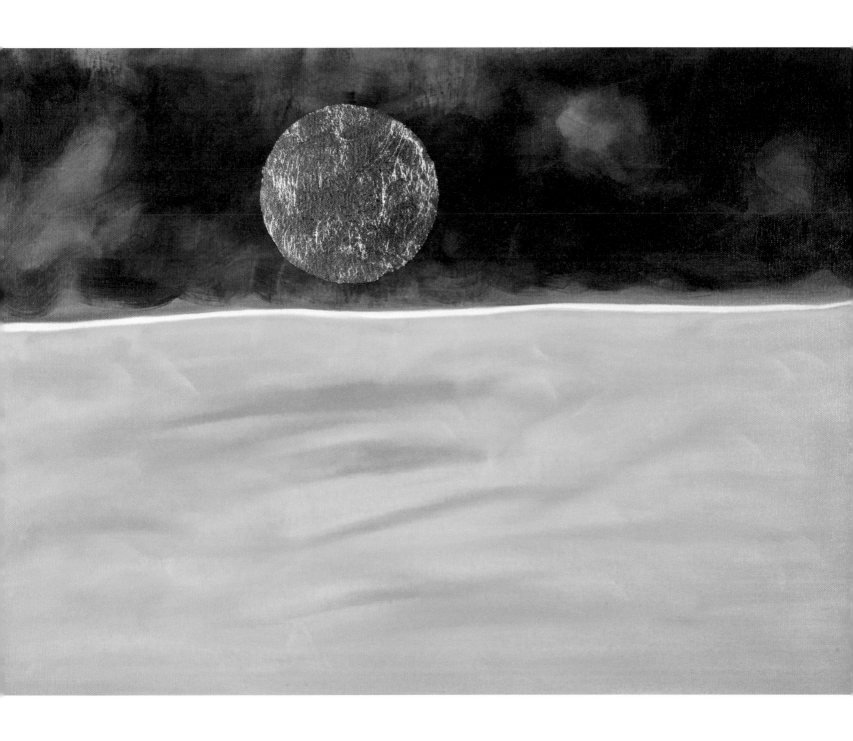

months, my challenge was to allow the paintings to create themselves. As I gained confidence and began to enjoy myself I marvelled at what was happening. I can't really interpret my paintings for you except to say that I think they have a lot to do with the land where I paint. The sun and moon or gold or silver is often the focus as I imagine that both have an enormous influence over our lives and how we behave.

Having always created in very simple, pared back ways I suddenly became excited by colour. Strong colour. My favourite painters are Patrick Scott, Mark Rothko and Monet through his water lilies, in that order. In Vermont I saw a huge red and orange painting by Rothko. It was hung in a huge, high space all on its own with a glass wall opposite. Outside was all snow and the brilliant light reflected from the snow onto the painting stopped me in my tracks. Wow, wow, wow.

Lauren had told me that Rothko painted in many layers to achieve his intensity of colour. I started putting up to twenty-five coats of paint on all or part of my canvases. I was often frustrated that I seemed unable to achieve the brilliance that I so desired. Recently, eight years later, revisiting those paintings I realise that I did a lot better than I thought at the time.

For a whole winter I painted in the freezing cold in a wood shed in Italy. There was a little creature between the size of a mouse and rat who would sit and watch me. She was adorable, with a little fringe like a baby's bonnet. At night she would sometimes climb onto the wet canvas to investigate. I left her foot prints the way they were as she was my first fan. After 9/11 I painted a series of two pyramids in the desert as my way of saying "Talk to these guys, they have been around for a long time". If you arbitrarily give part of Palestine to the Jews what do you expect? Particularly if you give Jewish Palestine a constant flow of arms. Talk, and talk real.

So far I have kept away from the whole gallery thing as my painting is very personal. I haven't painted for five years with all of my upheavals. I sense this is the year. I love painting, singing and writing. And that's only the beginning.

Back in Ireland, I decided to meet Declan Fearon of Tipperary Crystal to discuss the possibility that, instead of us having a rep each on the road going to the same shops, we might join forces. Declan was much more interested in my designing a range of glass for him. This scared and excited me. As we were getting to the stage of having samples made, the project suddenly slowed down. In the design game you know that this means that the client has lost interest. So I said to Declan, as you are losing interest and I am keen to go forward, please give me the details of the factory you use. He very kindly did and off with me. It was great fun. The factory would pick us up from the airport and there was usually someone from Waterford Glass or Tipperary on the Dublin flight. As the new kid on the block, I got my education on the two hour taxi drive to the glass factory. I was fortunate that the master glassmaker and head designer, Tihomir Tomic, was incredibly skilled and a gifted artist himself who has since become a close friend. A few years later at a trade fair in Frankfurt, he introduced me to a Polish glass company. Lauren, Tihomir and myself visited the factory and Tihomir showed the guys how to make some amazing big heavy art bowls for me. Then, while I was in the loo, Lauren designed a beautiful balloon wine glass with a single cut on it. I use one every day and it still gives me so much pleasure. When I saw the first sample I was afraid that it was too fine and delicate but customers loved it, just as I do.

Cathal Deavy, whose wife Dairin is the granddaughter of Dr J.B. Kearney, the very first collector of our pottery, was working in marketing for SuperValu and had the brainwave of doing an annual offer: one year four mugs, the next year four bowls, followed by dinner and then side plates. Market research apparently showed that if you mentioned my name fifty percent of the Irish population knew who I was. Then, if you showed people a piece of my pottery the number rose to sixty percent in Dublin and seventy percent in Cork. Based on this information, the quantity of pottery that Cathal required each year for five years was equivalent to double our current total production. I figured it was mad and so I said to Cathal that no I wouldn't do the pottery, but if either of us woke up in the middle of the night with another idea, let's talk. A week later Cathal called and said how about doing a set of sheets. I immediately agreed and the queen of market research, Colette Quinn, put in an afternoon of research at a hotel at Cork airport. Colette had a group of women of different ages and social backgrounds and the idea was to find out would people's love of my pottery carry over to sheets designed by me. The answer, to my surprise and delight was a resounding yes. I got the greatest ego boost of my life. I always knew that my pottery sold well but I had no idea what a warm place I had in so many people's hearts. These women were saying, "We'd love him to design other things." The linen promotion was one of the most successful SuperValu had ever had. Cathal subsequently left SuperValu and we have

Among the glass moulds.

Funny – this looks a bit like my pottery.

remained friends and he continues to give me great advice. I went on to do smooth, weighty stainless steel cutlery, glass, a rich, quilted bed throw and deep piled towels with Musgraves, but without Cathal I never had the same gas. I went to China twice during the cutlery project and once spent six hours with the technical head of production arguing millimetres and insisting that my initials went on the ends of each piece at an angle like the sloped back end of a yacht. The Chinese had to design a machine especially to do the stamp. The technical guy and his team stayed on especially to work with me while their buddies were outside letting off firecrackers for some holiday celebration. I was amazed that they were able to work to such exacting standards using machinery that was really medieval. On my way home I spent two days in Kowloon, Hong Kong, in a hotel up in the clouds in a tiny birds nest of a room overlooking the bay and the neon lights at night. The room was so small that any time I needed to turn around I had to go out into the corridor, and go back in again. From early morning to late at night I ate in a series of small restaurants and wandered the streets enjoying the oriental perfumes of food and people. A Pakistani guy on a corner persuaded me to go

Top: With Tihomir Tomic, learning my trade as a glass man.
Middle and Below: Relating my ideas to production methods.

209

to his tailor shop and offered me a shirt made to my own design for €80. I ended up getting six shirts for €80.

The sheets were a cakewalk. I started off with five very different options before the focus group. I was surprised and delighted that the ladies went for the simplest option, and then as we were leaving Helen Crotty (our Sales Manager, and much more besides) made a remark which cemented the whole thing in my mind. It was just a question of insisting on good quality cotton, which Cathal agreed with immediately. I really liked the simplicity of the pillow cases, duvet cover and sheets, but also the sense of luxury. Creamy, unbleached cotton with a satin finish and the same swirls that I use on my pottery subtly embroidered along one end. It just worked. In about three months my sheets turned over almost €4 million for SuperValu.

In the 1960s, I had a dream of designing for Dunnes Stores. It had nothing to do with money or exposure: I have an idea that my job in life is to bring beauty into the world. I also like putting a smile on your face. This is what motivates me. In the sixties the cutlery, pottery and stainless steel teapots in Dunnes were so depressing. When I visited less well off houses or hotels everything was depressing. I felt that we all deserved better and I knew that I could do it and that Dunnes Stores could be the perfect vehicle to make it happen. I suppose I was too much of a hippy to tackle Margaret Heffernan or her father. Just imagine me negotiating with the two smartest business heads in Ireland and you will realise why I didn't. I much prefer being down my leafy boreen making the pots I love, although there was a real buzz when containers of sheets started arriving into Musgraves. Maybe someday I'll have a go at fashion, although, it doesn't really fit in with my 'slow burn' philosophy of design. People still ring up looking for the sheets and the stainless steel cutlery. I do have an ambition to design an 'International Collection for the Home'. I would like to make as much as possible in Italy due to the incredible level of craftsmanship and the fact that most people I would be working with are in small family businesses like myself, and also so close to Ireland. S✿P

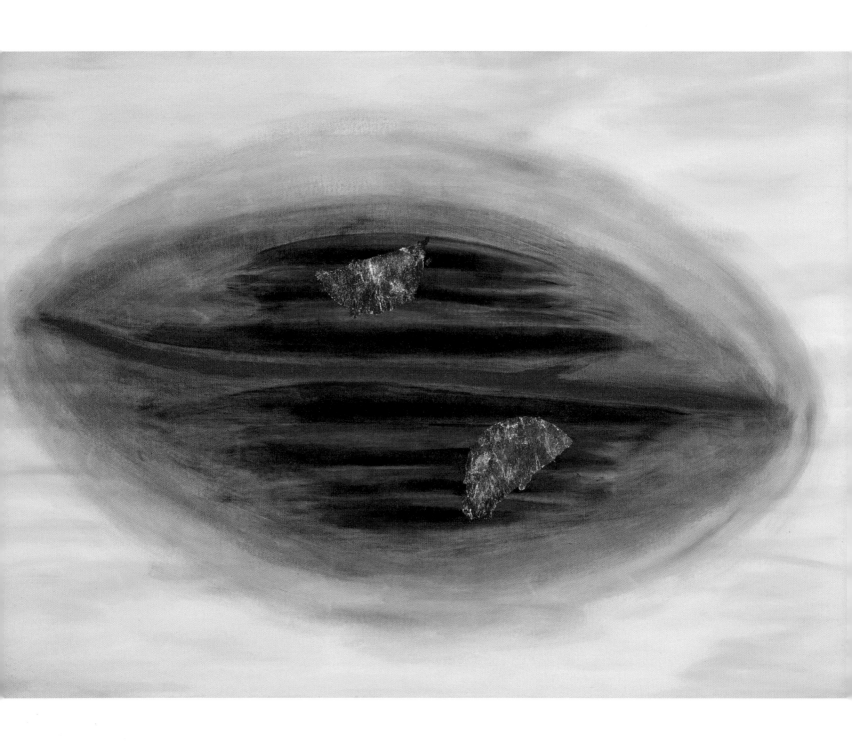

Playing with pastels.

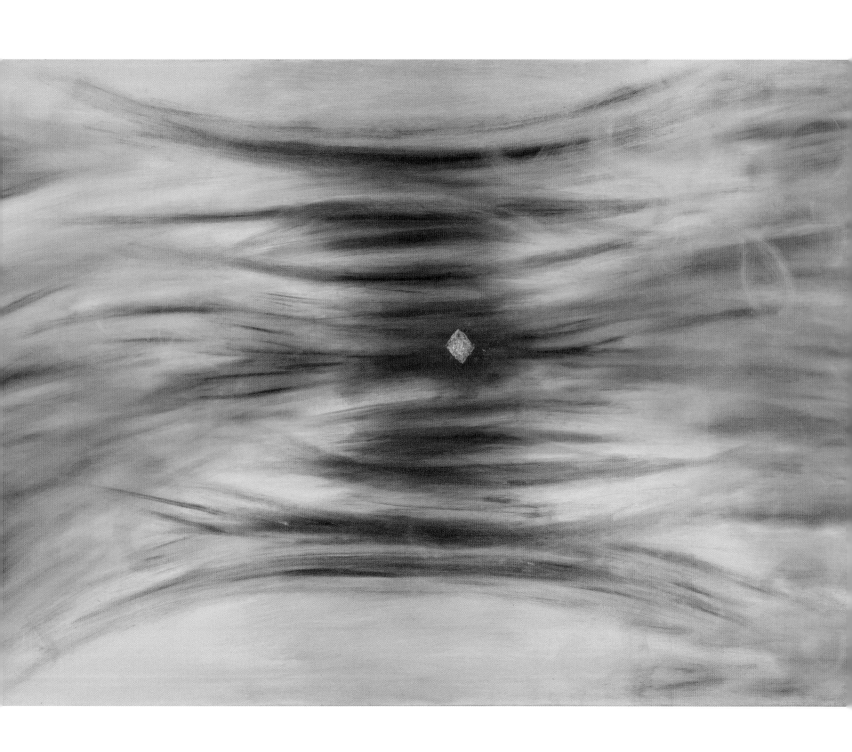

PART THREE
REVELATION

CRISIS &
CLOSING DOWN

"Keep your friends close, and your enemies closer."
Attributed to Sun Tzu.

By 2006 the Pottery was in chaos. Demand had been increasing year-on-year for almost twenty-five years. Part of our production was in my original Pottery building, the other part was in the Gallery building half a mile away, and the remainder was being done by John Walsh a couple of hundred yards away in an old hayshed. Half-made and finished pots were constantly on the move from one building to another and packing was a nightmare. One day I was down in the Gallery and one of our workers turned up on a forklift carrying a pallet with a small box on it. I enquired as to what might be in the small carton and was told it was a cake! Someone at the old Pottery had made it for the Gallery café and, rather than driving down themselves, had arranged for a forklift and driver to spend forty minutes delivering the cake. This is a classic example of a company in difficulties. I realised then that something had to be done to pull all operations together under one roof. There was just about enough space on a piece of land that I owned beside my original Pottery to put up a building that would be larger than all of the existing buildings put together. So in 2004 it was agreed to put up the new building. My only input was to make it big enough as I didn't want to be doing the same again in five or ten years time. There was also a massive kiln from Carrigaline that would have to be craned in before the roof went on and I didn't want to be ripping a roof off a few years down the road. Kilns are delicate pieces of equipment and I figured this one had done enough travelling. As it was, a specialist had to be brought over from England to supervise the move and testing of the kiln.

I really had no interest or part to play in the new building. I was starting to get nervous of the scale and nature of the Pottery. I like to have a relationship with the people working with me: now there were people whose names I didn't even know. At one point, between Shanagarry and Carrigaline, there were about 180 people for whom I was in a sense responsible for and I didn't even know them. In addition, the huge amount of money required for the new building began to shift the emphasis of the business from people and quality to making sure repayments were met.

At the same time as we opened the new building in the early noughties, sales began to slow down. It was like someone was turning off a tap just when we needed all of the water. The Celtic Tiger was booming and it never occurred to me that this was the beginning of a pattern. I just thought it was a blip, something that would end in a week or a month. But it continued. We had €4 to €6 million in retained profits so no one was too pushed at first. In hindsight, I can see that what we were experiencing was the beginning of an international insanity and global downward spiral.

Historically, because most of the world is poor, we all had a built-in caution around wasting things and over-spending. Remember the days when we saved up for things before buying them? In the early noughties we all went through a mental shift when it came to borrowing beyond our means, lustily encouraged by the banks. That is no excuse for us being foolish enough to buy into it. But it was becoming apparent that the banks were presenting inflated loans wrapped in red ribbons and sweet words and people all over the world lined up to buy the rubbish. For anyone who had gone through the mill trying to borrow from banks in the 1970s, 80s and 90s, it was like paradise had just arrived on an unimaginable scale. Every bone in my body knew it was a disaster waiting to happen and yet I joined the line outside the bank. Madness. Pure madness. I was too slow to read the signs and push through cost cutting measures. The stock was building to the point where we finally had more than six months worth of sales sitting on our shelves, yet they were giddy times and we were like kids let loose in a fairground. I suppose we thought that if we didn't enjoy it then it might stop or never come again (we were right about that bit). There is no doubt that I should have been at home talking to my customers. I just didn't feel comfortable around Shanagarry and the Pottery anymore, it no longer really represented what I had started. I felt I couldn't control it. It was slowing down and the debt was rising but I felt I had to keep going forward.

In January 2008, I showed my accounts to Donal Bolger of BLG who had previously advised me on my contract with SuperValu. At our first meeting after being introduced by my good friend Ruán Magan (the film producer and director who had just finished making a short film on the Pottery for me), Donal said to me, "I presume you have registered your name?" To which I replied it had never occurred to me. He gave me the address of Tomkins and sent me down to fill in the paperwork before we continued our discussion. For reasons that will become obvious later, thank you Donal.

If I was ever a celebrity it was not due to my talents with spreadsheets. Donal gasped when I showed him the figures for the Pottery. I should state here that I do not read accounts: I always ask someone who knows what they are doing. Years ago in the Pottery, we were signing off on the year's accounts and the accountant announced, "It has been a good year; you have made £40,000 profit." I said, "Show me the money." He said, "It doesn't exist." I said, "Don't ever mention profit to me again unless you can put the actual money on the table." My experience of life and numbers is that nothing is ever normal. There are always surprises both happy and unhappy. In accounts, when the columns of numbers go on for pages and end up being the exact same at the end to the nearest penny you know that somebody has been fiddling in the middle. There is no point in accounts to an amateur like me.

After due consideration, Donal said that I had to cut €200,000 from our costs for the year. I came back to Shanagarry to do my best, but that was a lot to cut. I had already taken a thirty-five percent cut in royalties. We did make an attempt. What I didn't understand at the time was the accelerator effect when a company starts haemorrhaging. On paper our stash of €6 million no longer existed and we were losing more than €1,000 a day which, for a company with massive overheads whose turnover had fallen to almost €1 million, was nuts.

On 21st July 2008 Donal Bolger called in for an emergency meeting. On the way into the meeting I said to Donal, "Well, at least we have cut a good bit off the expenses since you asked me to cut €200,000." Donal replied, "I'm sorry but from these present numbers you need to save €500,000 between now and Christmas." My heart sank. A fair effort had been made. I just had no idea of the size of the problem. I rang my brother Simon in the States that evening and he flew over immediately. I gave him the accounts and asked him how he would save the company. He went off for three hours and then we both sat down beside the fire together. I could see how upset he was, but I clung to the possibility of saving the Pottery. Simon steadied his voice and said, "Steve, there is only one thing to do. Close down the company as soon as possible; if not today then tomorrow." I said, "I need to think about it. Let's talk in the morning." He said again, "It's no good, you have to close it." I burst into tears and went to bed.

The next morning after breakfast, Simon again sat with me by the fire. Simon sat quietly for a moment and then said, "I know what you have been thinking all night." I was mentally and emotionally exhausted at this stage. "You've been trying to figure out how to save the Pottery", to which I replied, "Yes, and I think I have it worked out." He looked at me calmly and said, "Steve, would you stop. It's useless. The Pottery is gone. What we need to do is find the right people to help you do the best job possible from here on."

I called my accountant Conor Pyne. I spoke with a liquidator and I spoke with a solicitor. My first concern, once I knew that I had lost everything, was to make sure that the staff were taken care of. There were two terrible meetings with the staff. Terrible, because I felt such a fool and so useless. Luckily most of the staff had seen the end coming. I suppose if you were part of it every day for the previous three years, it was obvious. The first meeting was letting everyone know where we were at. The second meeting I brought two accountants with all of the paperwork. Everyone got as much time as they needed to sit down and have all their questions answered. They also received all of their documentation. I was terrified because the company had no access to any money. Luckily, in circumstances like that the State steps in. I suppose compared to the millions that the Pottery had contributed to the State, it was a thing of nothing. Well almost. I was in totally unknown territory and was very frightened. One thing I thought was very good and was relieved about was that at the time of closing my creditors and debtors balanced exactly, which means we must have been doing something right and that everyone should be paid off. I assumed that whoever took on the paperwork of the company would collect what was owed and pay that out to those that we owed and that it was a simple, clean transaction. I have since learnt that one Dublin company tried to pay nothing at all of what they owed; although eventually they did pay back some of it. Then somehow, under examinership, a fair bit of money got lost in the middle, and so to my great distress some people were left unpaid.

It is my opinion that the whole process of dealing with bankruptcy is legalised robbery. The further I got into the process the more I became gobsmacked at the standard of what any normal everyday person would call fair practice, decency or honesty. I have always trusted people. Now I can see how lucky I was not to be robbed blind years ago. I would like to sincerely thank all of the people in my life I've had dealings with who treated me fairly, honestly and with a generous spirit. That includes almost everyone before the Pottery went wrong. I remember a West Cork farmer saying to me as he handed me a cheque to invest in my first BES scheme. "I hope we will be the same good friends in five years time" (the date of pay back), and we were.

I used to have a joke which I can't use anymore. If I was in a solicitor's office doing up a contract and things started to get too bitty and finickity, I knew that either they were trying to write my downfall into the contract or they were trying to get me so bored that I would miss something that they were putting in. That's ok, big boys play big boys' games. My response to that crap was always, "Let's not bother with a contract, let's just shake hands on the deal." Looks of horror would appear and I would say, "You know what? I'm smart enough to make a living without stealing your money." They hated me for it because the implication was obvious. I like things to be out in the open. For me my word is my contract.

Having thought that I had some sort of grip on what was happening to me and around me, two high-powered accountants paid me a visit. They explained that things weren't as bad as they seemed and as I was a 'friend' and client of theirs they felt sure that they could find me an investor. Remember, this was September 2008. The shit hadn't really begun to hit the fan worldwide. In Ireland the banks were still open for business. If the Bank of Scotland in Dublin had accepted Dermot McHugh's (Joe McHugh's son, who was acting for the Bank) assessment of where I was, he could have saved me. But that is not where history went. There was talk of a six month global slow down, then two years and so it goes on, now maybe it's a further ten years because of the way the banks and governments of the world are behaving. The chaos could continue for another twenty years, who knows?

This is not a fiscal problem. It has been allowed to become a social problem. It is slowly dawning on people worldwide that their governments are incapable and irresponsible. Two things must happen to reverse the global downturn. Growth, modest growth must return and money must circulate. The sort of belt tightening that is going on is bullshit. The banks must be forced to play their part. As citizens we have bailed out the banks. Now they have received extensive funding, do they circulate the money? No.

My second point is that what is happening is all about people: pensions, hospitals, schools. We must be brought along, included and encouraged to participate in the re-energising of the planet. The whole situation is not about economics, it's about people. It's simple: people first, money and politics second. Anyone entering politics should have that statement branded on their ass with a white-hot branding iron. Charlie Haughey got his secretary to call me once to ask if I would stand for Fianna Fáil. I said let him call me and he'll find out. Charlie never called. They must have picked up the 'fuck off' in my voice!

The accountants went to court number six in the High Courts in Dublin on the 14th November 2008 and were given a number of weeks to find an investor under an examinership order from Judge Kelly. I was very impressed by what a grip the judge had on the nuts and bolts of where my company was at. I was also grateful for the space to breathe.

Losing the Pottery shook my very roots. I still find it quite difficult to talk about the aftershock. Although in going broke there are plenty of things that have to be done, there is also plenty of time for the mind to play games. If I had been younger and less sure of my relationship with my family, I would probably have ended my life. I constantly went over how I would do it. What stopped me was that I just couldn't figure out why my family should suffer and be left with the mess that I had created. My advice to anyone in the same position is to take your time and think it through. Ask yourself, is it really your best option? Forget your 'only' option. There are always options. Find someone to listen to you, and all the better if they are the type of person

Being with the one you love.

who will listen and not judge or try to advise you. For me it seemed like the soft option to avoid what lay ahead. I just couldn't square away leaving my wife to sort out the mess that I had created. Even now, five years later, I still haven't focused on what I lost in material terms. I can't see how getting into it would help. I see it like when a good friend dies. It would be great if it were not so but it is and therefore I must move on. Yes of course there are the odd quiet moments of thinking about Kevin Dunne (to whom this book is dedicated) and to all of my dreams of building an empire, but I have all of Kevin's photos to remind me of the good times and our friendship and I have such great memories of many other people and all that happened around the Pottery and my family.

Initially I was frozen stiff with terror. As the enormity of what had happened began to sink in, I would get angry at myself for being blind, for not acting sooner, for growing the Pottery so big. I have done a lot of work on my ego over the past thirty years and I imagined that I had a fair handle on it. But with the Pottery gone, there was my ego larger than my life itself. I find it very difficult recounting this to you. My mind is locked shut, I can't remember anything, my hand is shaking, my body is sweating and I want to cry. My tendency as a male is to change the subject before that last sentence. I find emotions dangerous territory for fear I might lose control and feel stupid. As a man I like to hide in a bunker, peering out through a narrow slit and only coming out emotionally when it's really safe to do so, which it rarely is. I felt useless, angry and helpless. I was terrified because I didn't have any idea what was ahead. Everything was taken out of my control. I was becoming angry at the way I was being treated by the examiner. I felt enormous sadness for losing the Pottery that my father had so lovingly started and then passed on to me. I felt useless for letting the staff down and was deeply concerned with how they were feeling. As a father and husband, I felt worthless. I have this male thing within me that says it is my job and duty to provide for and take care of my family. Now I could do nothing. I felt stupid, hopeless and very frightened. After all of the effort over the years building the business now, at six-ty-seven, I wanted to retire and enjoy the fruits of my labour. But there was nothing. I couldn't imagine where I would get the energy to start again. I searched for other possibilities to feed my family and pay my personal debts. It often got so bad that I would blank out and become almost zombie-like, functioning on a very basic level. Luckily, I had Lauren to listen to me, to support and help me through the dark moments. Thankfully, I didn't take to the drink or feel sorry for myself. Everything was so far beyond my ability to imagine that I just shuffled around in a daze; there was so much I didn't understand. Gradually, I began to realise that nothing would ever be the same again. Slowly, I decided that this might be an exciting new adventure. The universe, or God, in all of its wisdom would not set me a project that I could not achieve. In fact, I should be flattered to be set such a difficult task; God was honouring me. Somehow I managed to slowly raise myself out of it. I don't think I will ever completely lose the terror that still grips me sometimes in the wee hours of the morning. I now know that my family will be able to live off the Pottery some day in the future. Every step to rebuild has been accompanied by a worsening of people's ability to buy gifts and essentials, so it takes a lot of patience and resignation, which is the opposite to how I used to work. All my life I would see something that I wanted to do. Everyone would say it was impossible but I would do it anyway.

Throughout this difficult period I kept my eye on the people and children in makeshift hospitals in Libya, the refugees from Syria and Aung San Suu Kyi in Burma who had twenty years of her life stolen. I read the pain in their eyes and still they are going for it. Like me, the youthful exuberance is gone but life must go on. When I look at the endless ways that men, women and children the world over are wrongly suffering at the hands of their fellow humans, I know how very fortunate I am. I have hope and it will be difficult to take that away from me.

Time passed. Hours turned into days and weeks. From the confusion of just having had enough, I started to take small steps. I wasn't sleeping, I was crying a lot and my mind was a mess. I remembered my mother's advice when I was a teenager trying to get over love affairs. "Work hard, keep your mind occupied and everything passes," she would say. So whether I had slept at night or not, I would get up at six in the morning and three mornings a week I would go to the gym, which a very kind and thoughtful hotel manager offered me access to during this bleak time. I did that for three years. The question for me now though was whether to turn my back on pottery and follow some of my other interests. Having spent my life building my Pottery, I knew what hard work it was. Could I face it all again? Did I even have the energy anymore to do it? There I was living in my house less than fifty yards from my life's work. The examiner, having originally come down to help me, had switched sides, deserted me and evicted me from the Pottery on behalf of the bank for whom they then acted as receiver. Being locked out of my workshop by the people who were supposed to be helping me was tough. As if to intensify the loss the weather turned bitterly cold; it was the snowy, icy winter of 2009/10. During this period, a bidder had been allowed by the receiver into the old Pottery, without actually buying it. Between the examiner and the other guy, they cut off the electricity, telephone, gas and water to my house. Luckily, my good neighbour Thomas Beausang lent me a small diesel generator which I kept outside the backdoor and I put in a water pump. Tim Allen lent me some money and gave lots of supportive friendship. One morning, I went out in the snow at six o'clock to start the generator only to find that it had run out of diesel. I had nothing, no hot water, no light, no heat. The village was snowbound and everyone was asleep. I went into the house, lit a little fire and shivered and waited. At half past eight, I walked over to Beausangs'. Thomas came back with me with a can of diesel, bled the generator and away she went. I felt that things couldn't get any worse but that was a good thing: I had just about survived this far. Sages and mystics say that a big cause of our suffering is because we cling to things and people and that we believe we cannot be happy without them. Well I want to tell you that when I lit the fire that cold morning it was like an instant miracle. I was so much happier. I hadn't craved it. It was the only thing that I could do in my desperation and I was grateful for it.

Around this time I received unexpected gestures of loving, warm-hearted support both from friends and neighbours. Their kind, thoughtful and unobtrusive support touched my heart, made me feel humble and gave me a little faith at a time when I was so low. Thomas' generous neighbourliness; Margaret Casey, who had minded our showroom for years, dropped by and left me one of her husband's delicious smoked salmons; Pat Daly called to remind me of better times and with a plate of her lovely scones, and one evening I found a package with a selection of smoked fish and my favourite smoked eel with a message from Frank Hederman reminding me "This too shall pass". Sophie Lahive would pop in regularly to make sure I was alright, Myrtle Allen invited me frequently to dine with her, and Tim and Darina Allen were a giant rock of support. All such thoughtful and unexpected gestures meant the world to me in that time of despairing loss. I tried also to put my worries and fears in context. I was well aware of all the disasters going on in the world at the time. No matter how emotionally challenging it was for me, it was nothing compared to the suffering in many parts of the world, and so it was a question of minding myself and not becoming over indulgent. I thought, "I am not so badly off; I can surely handle this." I tried to put my anger at the receiver on hold and focused on whether I was going to continue the family pottery tradition that my father had started. Put like that, I began to warm to the idea. But how? The stress had a huge impact on me physically. Although I still imagine I'm a teenager, I don't have the boundless energy of ten years ago. The knees creak and I forget things. Then one day a timely reality check: a letter informing me that I was entitled to my free travel pass. In my wildest dreams I could not have guessed that I would have got such pleasure travelling by train from Midleton to Cork with a load of people my own age. But of course it was great.

Slowly and with time the total terror subsided and I began to sleep. I still found it very hard to concentrate for long periods and so I organised with Paddy Fitzpatrick that we would do a little gardening on fine days. Paddy had made pottery with my father and me for more than fifty years and he too was pretty miserable at the time. We raked leaves and slashed briars, cut logs and remembered the good times. I promised Paddy that he would have his job again and we joked about our youthful escapades. Then it came to me in a moment of nostalgia and stubbornness. I was not going to let anyone make me stop making pottery. My father had started the Pottery and I would honour him and myself by finishing the job and only ending if and when I chose. This clarity gave me great energy. The constant, positive, loving support I got at home from Lauren helped me steadily throughout all of this. She was great at checking in with me and asking how I was doing. She would encourage me to look at what I was feeling and to release it as a fear, often suggesting I just go for a walk to shift the energy. She made sure I minded my health and went for check-ups, gave me helpful, inspiring books to read and repeated often that yes, we could survive on very little without too many problems. Lauren also reminded me that ultimately the most important thing was that our kids were well and healthy and that we in ourselves were fine. I also want to thank my brother Simon, Paul McGowan and my solicitor Brendan Cunningham for supporting me unstintingly and for taking endless rambling phone calls from me and simply for always being there. Without them all, who knows?

I started to slowly realise that the process I was going through was one of the most important of my life, and that if I applied myself I could become a stronger, wiser person. Despite often acting the eejit, I have always hankered after wisdom. For years I had been on a spiritual path. I had learned to meditate in many different ways (which by the way is a mistake, it only confused me). I used to do winter and summer retreats with the Vietnamese Zen Buddhist monk Thich Nhat Hanh at Plum Village in France. Anthony de Mello, an Indian Jesuit who wrote *Awareness*, had been a big influence and now during this difficult time I listened repeatedly to Eckhart Tolle's *The Power of Now* as well as Byron Katy's *Loving What Is* on my iPod. All of these people are spiritual technicians who show us how we function mentally and emotionally. But, at the end of it all, one has to do it for oneself and then go on, and on, and on being vigilant as lazy habits are very addictive.

As the job of sorting out the Pottery went forward, I realised more and more that it was a sort of meditation and that the most important part of my life was yet to come. I didn't and don't know what that is or will be, but I'm excited by its prospect. I thought that over the years of study I had an understanding of and a grip on my ego. Oh how foolish I have been. My ego is like a flea in the bed. It just hides and bites at will. Why would I worry about losing the Pottery? I had built it once and now I had all of that experience to help build it again, if that is what I decided to do. I suppose that having reached the level of fame that I had, it would be surprising if I hadn't felt a bit important. But the feelings of total stupidity and utter loss that I felt were something that I wasn't prepared for. On the spiritual path, there is a thing called non-attachment. The idea is that any thing or person that we depend on for our happiness is a time bomb waiting to go off in our face. The great mystics have no possessions. I really thought that I was above and beyond worldly fame and possessions. Sure I like playing with my toys and I do interviews because the Pottery needs me to do them, but that's just part of my job. Oh foolish, foolish man. The only thing I will say in my favour – and I thank the universe for offering me the opportunity – is that I am not afraid to look and try to see what really is going on. I began to see my life before 2008 unwind like a video in front of me. I was amazed and appalled at many of the things that had got me to this point in my life and who I really was. I don't think I am a bad person. But I can see how often I have sleepwalked in the past. I remembered my spiritual mentor Don Rosenthal quoting to me almost twenty years ago a Russian called Gurdjieff who said that any man who looks deeply at himself and is not appalled has not truly looked. At the time, I remember thinking, "Oh yeah, another piece of spiritual bullshit, I am a fine person, I don't fall into that category." Oh foolish, foolish Stevie P. It doesn't mean that I am a bad person. It does mean that there are several games going on, on the same pitch, all at the same time. Watching the ball can be tricky but worth a shot.

My new self-doubt and lack of confidence had me asking myself over and over if I should go back to making pottery. I know how much work goes into setting up a Pottery. I know how much focus running a Pottery to the standard I demand of myself and everyone else takes. Will some of the old hands want to come back? At least I have almost fifty years of experience and wisdom gained from mistakes that I have made. While my head was spinning and saying, "Oh no, not again" another very real part of me was realising that I really like making pottery. I have a lot more to say in clay and I really missed all the kind people who visit my showroom and say nice things. In the end, rather than make a complete change in my life, I decided to return to what I know best.

I was going through an impossible time with the receiver. One day I am in a meeting with my solicitor at the receiver's office in Cork when I'm told that someone is interested in buying the Pottery and will I meet them? I am leaving the country the next day, so I tell them I'll be back in a month, set it up and send me a date for my diary. They explain that they would like me to meet the potential buyer that week. I felt like saying what you want is of absolutely no interest to me (bear in mind that at this stage the receiver was working for the bank and had no interest in me). But instead I said ok, I'll change my flight. You know you don't hold a lot of love and respect for an organisation which signs on to support and rescue you and then, without letting you know, turns around to destroy you. Someday, when I have nothing better to do I must enquire what the law is about such carry on, but for the moment it has to be constructive thoughts of onwards and upwards. I suppose what really makes me very angry about the receivership is that I behaved in a straightforward and honourable way during our relationship, whereas they were totally dishonest in every way.

When the day arrived to meet with the potential buyers I was expecting some ball-busting tycoons who wanted my name for nothing. Instead we had an easy lunch with a family team who wanted to get into pottery seriously. They knew that what my father and I had spent more than fifty years developing was

not just nothing. They also appreciated (the first people that year to do so) the value of my name, and that if I could be persuaded to be part of it the whole thing would fly. They also knew that in 2009 it was going to be very tough to start their own Pottery from scratch.

Because I know from years of experience that I am very good at running a Pottery and I have a clear idea of what my supporters want, I have always been very slow to allow anyone to influence me on how customers are treated and the quality and design of my pottery. I am softening a bit with age, but I really do need to trust who I am working with. Immediately I could see that my new partner was smart. I also felt that I could trust him and that we could work together. I had the idea that he would translate his life experience into pottery very well. This has proved to be very true.

After this first meeting I was happy, but still slightly nervous. I was about to let new people into my life because I really didn't feel like any more aggravation. I wanted to re-open a small personal Pottery, to re-connect with my friends and customers and to have no debt. Also, somewhere in the back of my mind, was the writing of this book. I have lived a very varied life with few limits and yet the Pottery has been a constant, even if it is steadily (and sometimes not so steadily) moving onwards. The Pottery is central to everything. Usually, in my life if I saw hard times coming, I would drop all distractions and circle the wagons around the Pottery. In a sense that is the way it was in 2008. Things had gotten so crazy that when Simon pointed out that I had hit a brick wall (and once I could see it) the only way to preserve the soul of the Pottery was to close it down. It might or it might not re-open but the chaos had to stop. I am sure that ninety percent of my staff wondered how it had taken me so long to see it: I suppose that's one disadvantage of being an optimist. You don't know when you're beat. But I did preserve the soul of the Pottery and it still lives and feels truer than ever. I was asking the journalist Barry Egan recently how he saw things so clearly from meeting someone only once. He told me that it is so much easier to see from the outside when you are not involved. As he said that, I saw myself in 2007/08 like a spider running around a web forgetting how it had been designed and built. Of course for a man, the possibility of stopping for a moment and saying, "Oh shit I am fucked," is very remote. S✤P

Ronnie Barrett accepting a suggestion graciously.

BACK FROM
THE BRINK

"It's too late to stop now."
Van Morrison

My new partner and I started to talk on the phone. He is a quiet, private person and prefers to stay in the background. I am the opposite. He put in a bid to the receiver for the Pottery and all of its buildings. I don't think he ever got a straight reply. We kept talking, and then the receiver decided to sell the Pottery to someone better known to them. At this stage I was out of Ireland most of the time, as being locked out of the Pottery and being treated like a piece of shit was not high on my list of wishes. Everything was very depressing and black. The receiver had wiped me off the map as a human being and, in my opinion, was stomping all over me. I got a top lawyer to advise me on how to protect my name and had to instruct the receiver to stop using it or anything branded by me and they had to comply. However, it didn't stop them from trying to sell several hundred thousand euro of pottery stock to someone for the total sum of one euro. They then let that person into the new Pottery building without any deposit. They put him out some time afterwards, only to let him back in again. A little more than a year later, they put him out once again for non-payment. In the midst of this circus I lost personal property and gifts from my father to me. Previously, I would not have believed this sort of behaviour possible from so-called professionals.

I had supported the receiver all along and gave them every help I could. I had got Ron Barrett, our best potter, to return to work at their request, making myself available, travelling at my own expense to any meeting they required of me and giving my technical expertise nearly daily to Ron, throughout the examinership and receivership. I simply wanted to ensure the Pottery was safe because basically it's always been about the best thing for the Pottery. It was a shock to realise that they were walking all over me.

The receiver asked me to return to Ireland to talk with another possible buyer. I told my partner that I would prefer to work with him, but he said that there was no harm in talking. I was on my first family holiday in five years at a friend's house and enjoying the tapas of San Sebastian when I had to rush to Biarritz airport and travel Ryanair to Cork. I met the other contender and the meeting was ok. We were walking out to his car and I remarked as we passed the old Pottery that I would really like to get it back as so much of my life had been poured into it. He retorted that he wanted it too and that he was going to get it. In my mind that was that, I could see where that relationship would go. I told my partner that whatever he and I might do, I would never work with the other guy. I did however have a few more conversations out of politeness for the receivership process, but I should have saved my breath.

The whole process of getting the Pottery up and running again felt like being a World War I tank floundering in a sea of mud with snipers shooting from all angles. In January 2010 I decided to return to Shanagarry and not move until something was sorted for better or for worse. I was mentally and emotionally way out of my depth but all sorts of wonderful friendship came to me including Mary Lambkin, the Professor of Marketing from UCD whom I had never met but who called me to offer her good offices in untangling the web. Mary has an uncanny knack for marketing and I could see how key that was going to be to re-opening in these difficult times. My partner and I kept talking and it became clearer and clearer that we would be in pottery together. It also became clear that the receiver would not sell us anything. They sold the old Pottery to the other guy and my partner had to negotiate a deal and pay over the odds to get the Pottery back. He has incredible patience and as I have said before, is very private. I often want to ask what's in his mind but he rarely says. For an old gossip like me that's strange but fortunately you don't need to be a good gossip to be a good partner.

I don't know whether it is legal or not, but the appointed receiver would not sell anything to me or

to anyone connected to me. There were pieces of land that belonged to me personally which had been used to secure loans: Pottery buildings, acres of Pottery land, the Castle, the Gallery. Everything sold for half nothing with no offer from me or my partner being entertained. I had no access to my own clay to restart. I couldn't get at my own personal equipment. In the end the clay, which belonged to me personally and was stored on my own unencumbered property, had to be moonlighted over to England for processing. I became very frustrated at how slowly negotiations were going and angry at how obstructive people were being towards me and my partner. Bless him, he just kept going. I couldn't have done it. He always appeared outwardly sure that we would get there, although I often wondered if that was really how he felt.

Eventually, after endless backward and forwarding like a county council steamroller, we were up and away. We started making pots in my old Pottery in late October 2010 and had our little showroom open on a very limited scale for the October bank holiday weekend. There had been a month of mayhem in the showroom. Absolutely everyone helped out while Ron, myself, John Walsh and Paddy Fitz led the way in getting production going. The place was like an unloved and filthy slum when we got it back. The kids all helped, but I think even they were a bit appalled by the sheer sordidness of the place. Lauren is very thorough and great at cleaning floors and my partner has a very orderly mind. If you ever need them I'll hire them out. Meanwhile, Cristin O'Reilly was flat out trying to figure out the numbers and getting the phone and gas reconnected; the power of course had been cut off for non-payment by the previous incumbent. I had a huge row with the phone company about getting my own phone and fax numbers back. The old company had supplied 200 outlets in Ireland but the phone numbers were still my personal ones in my name. I won eventually - and so I should have - but it was just another example of the fights I had to have. When we were all ready to go and Ron was on the wheel making his pots and John Walsh his curly bowls, I sent an SOS to Bridget O'Riordan who kindly came over and reminded me about all that I had forgotten about the showroom. I must admit, I did consider hijacking her but I knew that her husband would be over with a hurley.

When we opened those first weekends Lauren and Cristin gave out teas and coffees with barnbrack that Mirin had made, just as we used to do all those years ago when we first started. It gave a friendly, warm, personal and welcoming atmosphere to the place that had been missing and brought it back to the same cottage feel it used to have. Breda Fitzgerald from the old team came back to help in the showroom and it was great to see her familiar face and have her lovely garden flowers around the place. Her husband, Eddie and my brother had been best buddies at National school. I loved being out meeting people again in the showroom, particularly after what I had been through. There were wonderful well-wishers and a lot of genuine surprise that I had made it back. Ireland isn't very used to people who come back from the dead. I was so happy. I couldn't be up early enough to greet the pottery gang as we got production going again. Ron Barrett has been a tower of strength, both in organising and producing lots of pots. It gives me great pleasure to see him finally coming into his own, which the old structure didn't allow. Ron joined the Pottery in 1989. He very much trained himself as the Pottery was moving so fast that there wasn't any real training at that time. It was a bit like a traditional Irish family of a dozen kids, where the older ones take care of the younger ones. Ronnie is a very serious, honest, loyal, no nonsense man and he is a bit like me in that he is hardest on himself. At a time when the downstairs of the Gallery building was in chaos in the mid-1990s, Ronnie took it upon himself to take charge and bring order and control. As a result, some people resented him for doing such a great job. Thanks Ron, that's not the only time you have saved the ship. We should nickname you Captain and ask John Walsh (who is head of our local Land Sea Rescue team) to teach you to tie a few knots. Ron is making lots of wonderful pots now and receiving the credit and respect that he deserves. He also has two young daughters who run like the wind and who you will often see on the wheel themselves at weekends when Ron can't resist staying away from the Pottery.

Paddy Fitz of course was also there as he has been for most of the sixty years. Our relationship is still that of two teenagers. The old bodies are not the same, but the easy, deep friendship and appreciation is the same as when we would take turns singing a song in my father's Pottery in the late 1950s. I am not going to mention everyone as that is a book in itself, but I cannot omit John Walsh. John, like Ron, was always someone I could see great potential in but because the old Pottery had become so large it was very difficult to maintain close friendships. Now John has his own department and, instead of having moulds made in England and Italy, the mould makers have come to Shanagarry and taught John their techniques. Jeff Hand who led the charge of developing moulds in Stoke-on-Trent, expressed total disbelief at the speed with which John picked up his

Glass by Simon Pearce.

skills. I have to say Jeff, he had a great teacher. Thanks. Then there are the *Frattelli* Nencini from Montelupo near Florence (one of the most important centres of pottery production since the Middle Ages) who came to share their skills with John hardly speaking a word of English. I asked John on the first morning of them working together, "Can ye understand one another?" to which John replied, "Not a word, but can't I see what they're doing."

Unfortunately, Angela Treacy wasn't able to come back, though she did make us truly beautiful crib figures that first Christmas. I have a secret plot that sometime in the future we will get back together to revitalise the Gold range. Sadly, when I re-opened, Helen Crotty, who used to be a mainstay of the old Pottery and a long time family friend, had got another job and I didn't want to disturb her as I was flying on a wing and a prayer. I really miss having Helen around. Helen's grandparents and my parents were great pals. When, as a barefoot tousle-haired seven year old, I would call into their farm, the granny would always give me a 'googy egg' (as it was then called) to take home to my mother. I became very friendly with Helen's father Davey, a great mechanic, who was always buying second-hand machinery so that he could be fixing it on wet days. Davey had large strong hands and his hobby was sitting at the kitchen table fixing watches for everyone. When Helen was twelve, I met her one evening on her way home from her summer job of picking apples. I knew she was all flustered because her cheeks always went bright pink when she was bothered. "What are you up to?" I asked. She told me that she was picking apples for the summer so that she could buy a new bicycle. The problem was that she had just worked out that there wouldn't be enough money at the end of the summer to buy the bike. I said, "Helen don't mind the apples, come down to the Pottery for the summer and I promise you'll have your bike when you go back to school." Helen came every summer after that and became one of my best and most trusted friends.

It took me quite a few months after moving back into the old Pottery to feel at home again. It felt like it had been plundered and desecrated, which it had. Everything about the pottery itself, and my design work, is very personal to me. I always give my heart and soul to what I am doing and I'm sure, like Steve Jobs did, I often drive people around me crazy. "Wouldn't it be ok like this?" they say. No, it wouldn't. I'm designing it and it's going to be like this. It may sound very arrogant but in the design world you live and die by your ideas. So if you are going to die I'd rather the ideas were mine. I have no fear of taking responsibility for my actions. When the Pottery went bang I was the boss, the buck stopped with me and I paid the price. However, that was not the end of the story, it's just the beginning.

One day, soon after we re-opened, a woman came in, put €2,500 on the showroom counter and said, "Thank God you're back. I have been holding off buying my daughter her wedding present for two years hoping you would be." As I mentioned before, when the Pottery closed the goodwill started with my neighbours and friends calling in and leaving me little gifts. I received letters, cards and emails of regret and support that were very heartening, many from people I didn't know personally. Now cards and emails wishing us well poured in, and still do. I had kind messages from friends in the US that I have not heard from in almost fifty years. The good news is that I now have time to respond and remember wonderful days. The best was when I re-opened my showroom. Barry Egan and Brendan O'Connor of the *Sunday Independent* took me under their wing. Barry set the ball rolling and Brendan invited me on to his Saturday Night Show on RTÉ. One topic of the interview was suicide and I tried to share what was real for me and what I hoped people would empathise with. I saw one poor girl in the audience crying and the next week a young mother came to our showroom to support us and asked my wife to thank me for what I had said, but that sadly it was just too late for her husband who had gone a few weeks earlier. Please don't do it. From the bottom of my heart, please don't do it. There is always light and laughter. It may seem dark but there is always another option.

Every day, wonderful people come into my showroom and are so warm in their welcome back. There is a sea of good will out there. One woman who has a large collection of my pottery joked that she was sorry that I'm back as now she won't be able to sell her collection for a fortune on eBay! It really is extraordinary to me that something that started as simply and as humbly as my father's pottery has achieved such support and recognition, both in Ireland and across the globe.

When I returned in 2010, I decided to go right back to my roots where I feel most comfortable. The Pottery will stay small. You will always be greeted with a smile and hopefully a chat. The floors will be clean and shiny. Children are very welcome and if we have time, we will give them some clay to be experimenting with. In winter, there is always a fire and in the summer you can sit on one of our small garden terraces and enjoy a cup of tea, coffee or a glass of wine, and chill out. While standing talking to people when we re-opened, I realised that although there were a lot of former and new customers passing through the shop, there were very few bags going out the door. I watched people picking up the pieces and looking adoringly and then on seeing the price putting them down and walking out. Even though our 2010 prices were still the same as in 2008, they were too high in this new world. I spent a month driving everybody mad. "How many mugs do you make in an hour?" I would ask. "How long does it take to put handles on? How many fit in a kiln?" Then, in the office, "How much are the wages? How much goes on top for stamps and tax? How much are insurance rates, electricity, gas, boxes, packing materials?" The list went on. I began to wonder why I had gone back into the pottery. However, the good news was that after checking and re-checking – thank you Maura, Helen and Cristin – we saw a very interesting picture emerging which was that by running the Pottery as a cottage craft, rather than as an international corporation, the actual cost of production and overheads allowed us to cut our retail prices between thirty and forty percent. This delighted me because I too had to cut my cloth to suit my purse and I knew where most people were at. I know that many people love my pottery, but if you don't have money, you don't have money, end of story. That's just the way it is at the moment. For us, cutting the retail price is very tight, but I know it is for our friends and customers too, and since cutting prices the bags are flying out the door. It reminds me of my childhood. My mother bought very few objects, but what she did buy had real meaning to the family and lasted for years. After all, if the things in our house have meaning and feeling they really do make a house a home. In times like these, it really does make sense to only buy what you need and like.

I love simple shapes and unassuming pottery. I have been amazed in my life how many people have taken to my simple wares. Shops keep asking for colour and new designs though, but I move slowly and I like the idea that if you're collecting my pottery there is no rush, the same shapes will be there and if they aren't, which is unlikely, we'll make them for you. If it is a different person making them, they may be a bit different. Darina Allen has been very clever. She chooses only pieces made by Paddy Fitz so she has a long run of the same plates.

I have a very intuitive wife. I was saying recently that I am always surprised that I really love white. She pointed out that it wasn't surprising as, apart from that fact I love to pare things down to their essence, colour is often just fashionable for one season and if I followed fashion and changed colour every year then people couldn't go on collecting their sets. I met an Irish-American woman a few years ago whose job was predicting fashion colours three years in advance. Of course, it is mostly done by computers. This way, all of the fashion designers who buy into the idea can all be cool and use the same colour so that there is a theme. It sounds terribly boring and controlling to me. My dream is for everyone to have their own design sense and not to be over influenced by anyone. Maybe I should train you all as potters and sell you a wheel and clay and let you at it. Interestingly, my Celebration range of blue cornflowers has finally, after more than twenty-five years, come into its own and we are re-launching it by public demand. I have always been fond of it and I am delighted to think that it will find new homes. S&P

Make your own Masterpiece. Encouraging the next generation.

Above: Oran and Mirin happily eating ice-cream for a photo shoot.
Opposite: Two brothers. Photo Patrick Treacy.

THE NEW
NORMAL

"Don't worry. About a thing. Cause every-little-thing is gonna be alright."
Bob Marley

I must be one of the last movers and shakers to take the internet seriously. I believe I have achieved dinosaur status among my children. I really like talking to you. I look into your eyes and the story unfolds. I have always thought that a world of people sitting on their own with screens burning their eyes and communicating virtually was a sad state of affairs and sucks all of the juice out of life. However, I have finally seen that as a person who adores communicating, Facebook and Twitter and all the rest were made for me. Apart from the fact that I haven't learnt to be brief enough for Twitter, I am re-connecting with old friends and finding new relationships. It's great. Commercially, it's what I have always wanted. By far my most successful pottery outlet is my little showroom and Tea Room down our little leafy lane in Shanagarry. I can set the atmosphere. More and more each year, the shops that I supply are becoming stressed by their running costs and lack of real shopkeeping. Historically, there would be a supervisor for the China or Gift department and they would know which the best selling items were and order them regularly. Now it seems that retail is run by accountants who have a stock level for our pottery and only order when it reaches a magic number. Of course by that time the best selling items may have been out of stock for a month or more. Many shops with which I have had strong personal relationships for thirty years or more are becoming strangers as I am becoming just another number among the Chinese suppliers. Luckily the opposite is true among my customers. Because of the consideration and care we give to our customers, the only logical thing to do is to go head first into internet sales and nurture our relationships. Gift retailing in Ireland is in crisis. Retailers need to be creative and not be governed by their accountants. Retail is an exciting and vital activity. Running in fear will kill it and we will be left with only the internet; what a pity.

Patrick Treacy, Lucy's husband and a very close and dearly-loved member of our family, is in charge of growing our internet sales. Patrick is young, smart and sensitive. He is a scientist by trade but has chosen a different road. This seems to happen a lot in our family. My daughter Mirin is an ace mathematician and Ireland is crying out for maths experts but instead Mirin is off on a mountain meditating and fasting and chasing her soul. Patrick is quietly and patiently putting together what I believe to be the most important missing link in our Pottery; the ability to communicate with and supply efficiently and cost effectively any person anywhere on the planet in a way that they feel happy, honoured and respected. Patrick will do it I know. At the moment it is a time for meticulous preparation and deep thinking. We started well in 2011. 2012 saw a global shrinking of sales in our sector of the market, not too surprisingly given our on-going economic climate. We are preparing to be prepared for the future. I have every confidence. The one question is timescale. If you have any inside information please let me know.

Living every day of my life was one thing. Looking back over the past seventy years from here it's like a totally different life. Part of this is that wonderful hindsight which, if followed, would have made geniuses of all of us. The other leavening is that I was so busy rushing forward that I often wasn't that present and so I only partially tasted what was happening. I'm amazed now at the really important bits that I missed at the time and the bits that I noticed but chose to ignore. Chief among my not 'seeing' was my relationship with my brother.

Simon and I have a similar core but a very different way of expressing it. When I was three and Simon arrived in our family, it was nothing but an inconvenience to me. We had a great little family and I was the focus of all attention and then this guy comes along. No matter how skilled parents are, there is no accounting for the irrational idea (which seemed totally rational at the time) that goes on in the older brother's head. After a few years it was handy to have someone to play with. Then he started, as he saw it, being part of projects, and as I saw it, wrecking things. You know boys. We kind of split up and went our own ways, although I knew Simon adored me, which annoyed me and I often press ganged him into helping me with other projects. Poor Simon, I was really very hard on him. At boarding school, when I was about fourteen and Simon about eleven, he really thought I was very successful. I was going through hell. All head stuff, but what goes on in the head, though not real, can seem very real. My impression was that things seemed to flow much more smoothly for Simon. He seemed very self-contained in his occupations like shooting ducks, motorbikes and hanging out. Our parents always assumed that Simon would be very successful in making money and that I would just be. I always insisted on making my life very difficult. I was always in a hurry to get things done. I was not good at respecting that Simon had his own path. When I met Simon in Tokyo in 1966, I was so happy to see him. It was incredible. But I soon fell into my older brother control mode. Biology is a bitch. I do take responsibility for my life but some habits are very hard to shake. I have watched many farming families where the eldest son assumes that he is entitled to the farm and however hard the younger son works, he gets little or nothing in material terms. I was part of that headset. I was in total awe of Simon when he went off to make glass in Kilkenny. I was jealous of him when he went to America in 1979. I considered moving over to be near him: America is just not my speed. Currently, after many ups and downs on my part, I think that I have found a balance with my brother. Simon and his lovely wife Pia have been extraordinarily generous to me and my family through these past few difficult years and I hope I have matured enough never to row with him again. I think he knows that I really do love him.

From being a long-haired, disorganised hippy, I reached a certain point where I had money and power to do many things. It's as if there were two people in me. I always really like just quietly doing things

with my hands. I envied the Irish farmers of my youth who had lots of time in the winter to do bits of building and fix machinery or make furniture and chat to their friends by the fire. That is who I would like to be as a potter. However, there is this lunatic force within me that drives me to achieve things such as power and money and to show how clever I am having created such huge projects. I have always driven myself to exhaustion. Maybe this is our life's work, to get to know our real selves. In that light, losing the Pottery and lots of money was a very good thing as I now have the time and inclination to get to know myself and my friends better. I am still an erratic hippy (without the hair). By looking at myself straight in the face, I'm starting to see who is there, who has been there all along and that his real needs are challenging. I know I can do it but I am amazed at how many surprises I am getting along the way.

For one moment, I would like to project my vision out into the world. As for me, so for Ireland, we both went off the tracks in the early 2000s, but it doesn't stop there, almost every person and country on the planet has done it. Now is the time to stop and take stock and completely change the way humans run the planet. We have to do it. Even in the days of the British Empire there was wiggle room. Now there is none. It's survive or don't survive. We must act. In today's world, money and major corporations rule. I am not a solicitor or a communist and have ceased being a capitalist because it doesn't work. I am a human being. I am sure that like me you are looking around gobsmacked at the global stupidity. But it is a bit worse than that. The wealth and power to control us is in the hands of a very few and among these few greed is rampant. We have all read for years that the rich are getting richer and the poor poorer. Until recently, I didn't take any notice because I presumed that sanity would prevail. I was wrong, greed is prevailing and in the hands of an unscrupulous few. This is not the place to go more deeply into this issue. I must end with my convictions, my faith and my trust in our human spirit to survive and to create a fair and bountiful planet with justice and caring and love. That's the future I see, and I see the urgency. Good luck on your journey. I will just continue to bring beauty into your life, that's my job. **S*P**

Opposite: Mirin checking quality.

FAMILY

"Love is definitely a kind of madness."
Gerald Pringle

I walked into a room in Dublin and there she was, a vision. Bangles all up her arms and a cheeky smile. A siren. I hit the rocks immediately. Not even a moment's hesitation: bang and it was all over. I was like clay in her hands, the will to fight, the desire, evaporated. What bliss. But I wondered how she felt, so I asked her for a hug. She gave me one. Then I said that will do for ten minutes, setting myself up for the next. She was deeply offended that I thought the effect of her hug would only last such a short time. I invited her to dine with my godfather and she said yes. In the middle of dinner, not having managed to say anything at all, I grabbed my chance while my godfather had slipped out of the room and asked her, "Would you care to come to Japan with me in the spring to view the cherry blossom?" Lauren said yes. She was great at saying yes, when she meant it. I have never understood the advantage that many women see in saying no. We went to Cork, night turned into day and day into night; the romance of it all. She would arrive in Cork on the Friday evening laden down with exotic cheeses and handmade Florentines. Both of us enjoyed cooking and drinking wine by the open log fire. I have never met another woman with her sense of style and intelligence. With the part of her that has travelled from Saigon (she is half Vietnamese) there is a ferocious determination and physical strength. What a cocktail. It was four years after first meeting Lauren that we finally got to Japan to view the cherry blossom along with our baby daughter Mirin. Mirin was born in 1991, the day the Soviet Union split up. We wanted to name her Mir, the Russian for 'peace' as her coming brought peace to our own lives and we thought we'd give the Russians a leg up in their new adventure. Hence 'Mirin' (which is also Japanese for 'sweet sake').

Lauren has a phobia of hospitals and even Dr Edgar Ritchie his wonderful team found it difficult to get her to offer up Mirin. It seemed to go on for days and Lauren was totally exhausted. Fortunately, everything finally worked out. Two years later in 1993, Lauren insisted on a natural home birth and engaged a wonderful midwife, Betty O'Toole, whose care of Lauren, before, during and after the birth was phenomenal. She also went to Dr Pallany Pillay who now had his own very welcoming and homely City General Hospital in Cork. Unusually for most doctors in his line of business, Dr Pillay put off his summer holiday to be there for our son's birth. Two weeks before the due date, Lauren felt sure she could and would have a home birth. Knowing that Dr Pillay had offered up his summer holidays, and also that the VHI, which wasn't interested in natural birth, refused to recognise Dr Pillay's hospital, I called Dr Pillay and explained that Lauren was going to have a home birth but that our original contract stood and I would pay him the agreed amount and that I would still like him to be available on the day. Hopefully, he would be paid for doing nothing. It is worth noting that for me having the woman I love deliver a baby at home was terrifying. Lauren ordered a birthing pool in which she hoped to relax as needed. Betty came promptly when called, and using natural techniques and shiatsu, soothed Lauren along. I lit a huge log fire in the sitting room and set up the pool, filling it with hot water. The water thermometer was in the shape of a fish and as soon as our little two year old daughter Mirin saw it she leapt up into the pool to play with it. Lauren and Betty went out into the garden in the warm sun. When they came in Lauren decided she could do with a little relax in the pool. I decided to show some solidarity and undressed except for my boxer shorts and helped her into the pool. Next thing I could see a head appearing. As a male I am totally phased. The head seemed to me to be blue, underwater and not breathing. I yelled, "Betty, get your ass in here", but she calmly replied that she was making tea and that I could handle it. Suddenly, out popped Oran. When Betty arrived with tea and we cut the umbilical cord, Oran was beginning to start his new journey in life. Lauren wanted to call him Jhett (which is in his name) but we settled on 'Oran', a third century saint from the West of Ireland.

Don Rosenthal and his wife Martha have spent a lifetime investigating and looking at the spiritual path. One focus of their journey is the glue that holds relationships together. Having spent a lot of time and energy upping the quality of their own relationship, they hold weekend retreats to share their knowledge and experience. My brother Simon and his wife Pia went one weekend, and as soon as it ended, called us and recommended that Lauren and I give it a shot. We learned a lot of very obvious and simple things that on our own we had missed, even though we had what we thought of as an already deeply loving relationship. We became firm friends with them and Don and I have spent time together in Shanagarry as well as on retreats in very remote places. Don, being able to see right to the core of matters, has the gift of seeing things that are hindering me in my life and then allows me to discover for myself what it is that might be helpful.

One evening in 1997, Don and I were in my Japanese Tea House in Shanagarry. Having spent several days doing what we call 'hanging out', which is meditating and discussing all sorts of things to do with life and relationship, out of the blue Don asked me, "Have you ever thought of marrying Lauren?" As Lauren and I had both been married once before it was not on the top of either of our agendas. We had been together, blissfully happy for ten years, made babies and life was fine. Why complicate matters? I replied that we had no plans but that I had always made it clear to Lauren that if she wanted to get married to let me know because I was open to the idea. Don looked at me like he had seen a ghost. I suppose we had both assumed that I was smarter than that. Don said, "Stephen, you don't understand women. No woman is going to respond to that reasonable, unemotional line of yours. You need to sit down with Lauren, and while looking her straight in the eyes, say something from your heart like, 'You know I love you very much and I would very much like to marry you. Will you do me the honour?'" I said, "Don, you're joking!" I couldn't believe I was so off the tracks. With Don's prompting, I realised that I had been caught up with the male fear of commitment, but that actually the deep love I feel for Lauren goes so much deeper than that. He suggested I go and get Lauren so we could try it out. I went and invited Lauren to join us in the Tea House. We sat on the floor and I asked her. She gave me a big hug, burst into tears and said yes. Don married us the next day in the Tea House and it was one of the most special, gentle, and profound ceremonies of my life. We both regard that as our real spiritual marriage. That morning, we didn't tell anyone what was happening, but I asked Lauren's mother, Kim Vo, if she would kindly prepare us one of her Vietnamese suppers, simply saying we had a couple of friends coming over. Why didn't we tell Lauren's mother? Well you know the way it is with us men and mothers-in-law. I just didn't want to go through the reasons for having a 'proper' wedding for her only daughter and Lauren didn't want her mother to tire herself out making a Vietnamese wedding feast, which she would happily have done had she known; she was such an amazing cook. When we announced our marriage to everyone at the dinner, after her initial disbelief, Kim Vo was very supportive and laughed at the idea that she had unknowingly cooked our wedding meal. It was truly delicious and Don was in great form. The following year we married 'officially' in Florence in the Palazzo Signoria with just a few of our very close friends and family and our two small children, but our ceremony in the Tea House is the important one for us.

Mirin and Oran are now in their early twenties. Both young adults, they are developing into very individual people with very strong values and consciences with regard to our planet. Both are creative. Mirin will turn her hand to anything and make it flower. For a period when we first re-opened, she worked in our showroom and then ran our little Tea Room devising and cooking up a storm of delicious lunches while also making unusual pieces of jewellery. As children, I tried to show Oran and Mirin how to make pottery, but they insisted on being left alone to figure it out. By the time Oran was seventeen, he had been learning secretly, late at night and really has something very strong to say. Oran's pots are very individual and though he uses the same black and white glaze as we do in our Shanagarry range, he does so in a distinctive way. Interestingly, some of his mugs remind me of my father's early pieces. In the autumn of 2010, Oran started to sell a few of his pots in our showroom, though he refused to have anything to do with the Pottery itself. He made his pots, glazed them and his sister sold them for him. Mirin also makes great pots. I regret being so busy building my empire when they were young, though Lauren gave them the earth mothering they needed in spades. Mirin now comfortably speaks Italian, French and Spanish with a few words of Japanese. Oran has Italian and French, and apart from pottery, is a musician and a serious snowboarder chasing the snow whenever, and in whatever country, he can. It's hard work getting to know people in their late teens and early twenties, but I am quietly getting under their skin a bit. I am so happy that they are such individual people. Every child is. With Oran and Mirin, they feel that they have full permission to explore their own individuality. Where I have spent years trying to be at one with the spiritual side of my essence and to just be present and conscious and living in

the moment, they seem to simply and naturally be living and doing it.

Two monkeys.

My eldest daughter Lucy is now in her thirties and married to Patrick Treacy. They have three adorable children. Timmy is eight and the image of his mother at that age. Merrily is five and Aisling is three. I find it extraordinary the way my children have all continued on where their grandparents left off. I suppose my spirit is there but I see them in the light of my parents. Lucy, having published two books is on her third (and fourth!) and has created, hung and sold an exhibition of unique paintings. She blogs endlessly, edits and contributes to magazines. Her passions are women and their creative potential, how to upgrade and update their lives, and child-rearing. Lucy always finds different ways of examining and throwing new light on accepted values and beliefs. I'm a hard goer but Lucy leaves me dizzy. Many think she has cracked the secret of supermum, and she is definitely working on it but, sometimes when we share a coffee, I see a little tear of exhaustion and frustration from children who think that the night is for partying.

I don't look into the future or past very much. I find it a full-time job living for today. The other night before going to bed, I promised myself that I would draw a conclusion to this conversation. I have given you a small sample of the flavour of my life. This is my 70th year and the diamond jubilee of making my first pot and my father starting Shanagarry Pottery. I would like to end by expressing my love and respect for my father, something I have never done before as I was often so focused on my mother.

Most days I rise from bed before dawn, and on this wild winter's morning, the first thing I do is light the fire with some logs which I

cut from a fallen oak of more than a hundred years old. Last night, over a glass of red wine by yesterday's fire Patrick told me that his son Timmy (my grandson) gets up every morning and lights a fire for him. I used to do that for my parents at that age. Maybe it is the family meditation. Certainly, I became clear about what I want to say to you as I drew out the night's embers and placed them on today's sticks. The wind is howling outside and the rain is lashing against the window. I have an image that the journey of our life is like a huge roll of magic carpet that we find when we are born. We playfully start to unroll in it. It goes over scented rose beds, down muddy laneways and across parched deserts. The carpet is endless. It is your carpet, but the most fun is when we share it and allow other people to walk on it. It is really important to keep on unrolling it across the landscape which is not of our choosing, but which we can explore with courage.

The idea that every thought that we think, and every action that we take, effects and influences everybody and everything else, makes sense to me. It gives conscience a purpose and gives our lives an incredible potential and deep meaning. Not so long ago in Europe, most human activity was on a modest scale based on small groups of individuals: bread makers, tailors, blacksmiths, weavers, and farmers. There are plenty of good reasons why these small enterprises flourished and worked together without government handouts. I started out as one of these. I made the mistake of growing my Pottery to the point where I didn't know many of the people within it, and in the process lost the rest because I lost sight of my guiding principle: the need and desire to empower the people around me. I am not a businessman, but an educator by example. For me, lighting and minding a

Opposite: The complete family after our Tea House wedding ceremony.

fire, and feeling a piece of wood or clay take shape in my hands, brings life to my body. A true educator shares their experience because it makes them feel alive. To truly educate others is to find your own path and to give thanks for what you have received.

We are now in a place where governments, religion, bureaucracy and banks control everything. But the world and its people are waking up to the realisation that the engine that drives every country is small activities. They create work and wealth in a community. For the last three years, sixty-five thousand small enterprises per year have been forced to close in France alone. If you look anywhere in Europe it's the same story. As someone on the frontline, I can tell you that I would not advise my children to become crafts people, and yet they probably will because it is a very natural expression of human endeavour. A government's job should be to create a context for society, then let society get on with it. Nowadays, my main competitor for potters is the social services. I am proud to live in a Europe where there are safety nets. However, when those services give a sense of individuals not needing to take total responsibility for their lives, it is contrary to human nature. We need to struggle; it's important. But we do not need to starve or freeze or have our heads wrecked by bureaucracy. The satisfaction in struggling and succeeding is my drug of choice. For me, struggling is the opposite of gambling. In gambling you continually double your bets to cover your losses and eventually lose. In struggling with life, if you focus and stay wide awake, there is always a gap in the clouds for the sun to shine through. At least that is my experience.

My father Philip was a gentle man. He never hit me, nor tried to impose his will or ideas upon me. He was always like a shadow in the background of our family and yet his influence was always there in a subtle way. If I ever gave out or complained about my father's ways, my mother would always remind me that I had a lot to be thankful for in my father. "It is because of him that you have so much freedom," she would say. I couldn't see it then, but now more than fifty-five years later, I know she was right. He lived in a deep, quiet, spiritual place. On the surface he worried about money and often seemed ineffectual. He dedicated the second forty years of his life to making pottery and listening to classical music. Was he content? I don't know. But I like to think he was. Soon after my mother died and I had left home, Philip had a stroke. His recovery was largely due to his stubborn determination and the help of a loving friend. He continued to wear his signature beret, half over one eye, only now his left arm was in a sling. He still found the energy and gusto to tear down our boreen in his brand new fast car.

One evening, having driven down to Dublin in the morning to see his new girlfriend, he was flying along a back road on his way home. He fell asleep and the car took off over a ditch through a tree and landed in a field right way up. A local Garda was passing and drove the car out of the field to the pub about 200 yards away. I was called out and there was Philip sitting a bit muddled in front of a roaring fire with a glass of whiskey in his hand. The wisdom was that if he had a whiskey in the pub and was later breathalysed it could be said that he was driving sober (which he was) and that he had had a whiskey to steady his nerves after the shock.

Philip had very much his own take on life. He was very good and patient with me and I knew he was always there for me, even if I didn't always have a lot of time for him. I was mammy's boy. Philip's recovery from his stroke was largely due to his stubborn determination. A few years later he remarried. I had great difficulty adjusting to the new situation as I felt that my sister Sarah and I were no longer part of this new family. In my attempts to deal with these emotions, I became very angry. I worked hard at trying to bridge what I saw as the gap, but because of my anger, I went about it all wrong. Eventually, Philip lost his memory and didn't know who I was. One fine, cold, autumn evening I went up to his bedroom. There he was sitting up in bed looking out at the bright evening light shining on ponds of water and birds coming in to land in the rushes. He was smiling and lucid and we sat and chatted in a way we hadn't in years. Philip always talked part in abstraction, part in the present. As I was going out of the door he said with gentle force, "I am so grateful to have come to Shanagarry, everyone has been so kind to me and it has been such a full and happy life." I walked home literally bouncing off the ground, so happy that my father was back like before. Not for a moment did it enter my head that often just before death people have a moment of great clarity. At six o'clock the next morning the night nurse called me to say that he was dying. I ran the hundred yards to his bedside and held his hand as the last breath passed out of his body. Then just stillness. It's like nature needed a few moments to punctuate the last sentence.

He left me his Pottery which was in fair chaos and worthless, except to me. I was determined to return it to its former glory. I recalled all of the stock that shops held because of poor quality. Unfortunately,

Mirin making an ashtray!
Photo Patrick Treacy.

Patrick Treacy and Lucy Pearce on their wedding day. Photo Lauren Pearce.

STEPHEN PEARCE, POTTER

Left to right: Simon, Lucy, Stephen, Oran, Simon's son Adam, Mirin. In front: Lucy and Patrick's children Timmy, Aisling and Merrily. Photo Patrick Treacy.

the damage had been done and between 1993 and 2008, I only managed to get Philip's black and white Shanagarry range up to fifteen percent of our total output. However, since re-opening in 2010, it now sells almost fifty percent of our output. I always made my relationship with my father difficult. Luckily, in writing this I have finally cemented the true love which we bore for one another. Thanks Lauren, as without several nudges from my wife I don't think I would have gone there and completed the emotional journey and the story of our pottery. The need for space to produce the Shanagarry range was one of the reasons for developing the Castle. Penn Castle was to be the continuation of my mother's life's work. The fact that the Catholic Church prevented my Learning Centre gave me the gift of facing my anger head on. In turn, I lost the monster that the Pottery had become and was forced to check in on my values and choose to take ten paces backwards to where I started. In doing this, I have become closer to you my friends and to my customers and so have decided to share my life and adventures with you all. I'm far from finishing my journey, but I do feel whole and purposeful at this moment. Never give up.

I think I have lived a very blessed life. I have often made it hard going for myself. I have definitely created more good luck than bad luck. I have struggled with spiritual matters, which to me are the only game in town. Whenever I have needed a hand of friendship, it has been there for me. I love the human race and I marvel at our collective stupidity. When you consider that we are each pieces of God with unlimited potential, our choices are often pure soap opera. If only we could really understand that we are individually totally responsible for every choice we make, and that every choice we make affects everyone and everything in Creation. Some game, some power, some choice. If every choice we make comes from our heart with love, then heaven can be here for us now. It is here anyway but do we need to choose it for ourselves? I have tried to illustrate through my life and pottery the hope that I have for us all. Please mind it with love and don't forget to love yourself.

The End (or is it just the beginning?) S&P

POSTSCRIPT

Oran and his godfather, Kevin Dunne, 1998

As an illustration of where things have travelled since my gentle philosopher father, I will leave you with an email I received from my son Oran at Christmas. I suppose if it's in your genes it's in your genes. However, you still have to look, see, feel and express it.

My email to Oran, who is living with his dog meditating and writing music said, "Hello. I am S. I know that you are O, but I don't know you very well. For that matter, I don't seem to know S that well either. Maybe you could help me to get to know S a bit better? Of course I'd love to know O too." The reply from Oran came back. Thank you universe for giving me so much. Thank you Stephen for recognising the gifts and picking them up. Thank you all for sharing them with me.

Hello. This strange thing seems to happen in our universe; time speeds up, and accelerates, for infinity. As time speeds up, things start to get more complex, in a day now we can experience more change than would have been experienced in thousands of years a while back... as far as we know. In all this complexion, and in an attempt to reverse time, I seem to have forgotten about emailing. So hello. You are this universe. You are also any universe that is parallel or in any way linked to this one. Which I assume is every universe and thing that exists. You are infinity, therefore you will never die; your energy will combine with others to bring renewal and rebirth of yourself, when you are ready. With that comes infinitely limitless possibilities, you are all possibilities, anything that can be imagined. We are colourful energy, that is a manifestation of pure love; a consistently inconsistent, paradoxical spiritual soul of infinitely limitless consciousness. More importantly to this life, we are children of a planet that we call Earth. We are the world. We hold all the potential and possibilities for our mother earth, and boundaries do not exist. We can be and do whatever we want knowing that what we do to others is exactly the same as what we do to ourselves; for we are one big consciousness, a whole. What happens to one, happens to the whole. There aren't lots of different beings experiencing consciousness, there is one being, experiencing one consciousness through infinite different paradoxical expressions of love. How we choose to share this love for the one source, is who we are in this life. Same thing as karma really, our consciousness will continue to bring forth the learning experiences that we need for our soul, until we fully feel it to be our truth by surrendering to our spiritual love and all possibilities. Then we can share what we have learnt, in whatever way inspires us. We are all the same source, we have all taken different streams to explore and experience, flowing with or against the river, until finally we surrender to its divine magic which brings us to the ocean where we finally realise that we are all connected and the same one source. We are all that ever has, and all that ever will be. Namaste, Jah Rastafari.

ACKNOWLEDGEMENTS

It would be impossible for me to thank you enough, my friends, my family and of course my customers, for your support in making my Pottery possible. Thank you from the bottom of my heart.

In a forest trees grow tall and straight, thanks to their friends around them.

That has been my life.

So many hands of friendship. So many loving gifts. Where do I start? Definitely with Lauren. I wrote this book longhand at the kitchen table. Lauren put it into the laptop, correcting spellings, suggesting bits I had forgotten, reminding me that my anger doesn't belong in this book. Editing and choosing photographs and then matching photos with text. Three times she stopped me from throwing the whole lot on the fire. So no Lauren, no book. Thanks. I am delighted by the result of our labours.

Niamh McSweeney did the first edit with courage and conviction. My brief was that we should end up with a fireside chat and not a learned tome.

Whenever a gap appeared in the chain Patrick Treacy patiently fixed computers, retrieved lost gems, sorted photos and finally checked punctuation, spelling, missing words and sneaked in the odd sentence.

Brian Wilson and I agreed typeface, size, colour paper and general layout. Then Lauren chose from Kevin's photos and raided family boxes in the attic. Brian laid out the pages and finally put everything together.

Vanessa O'Reilly cleaned, dusted and touched up hundreds of negatives and put them all on high resolution discs.

That's the A team six people. For encouragement and an insight into the publishing world I would like to thank Antony Farrell of Lilliput Press and Fergal Tobin of Gill & Macmillan. Though they couldn't see this book working for them they most generously pointed me in the right direction.

My daughter Lucy, Donal Musgrave, Antony Farrell, Fergal Tobin and Mary O'Sullivan all read the original text and graciously didn't show horror. Lisa Clifford read the almost final version and over a couple of beers and we put it to bed. Ruan Magan and Colette Quinn listened to me in confusion and wisely said nothing. Franco Ancilli through his broken English and my broken Italian walked me through the production process with endless patience whilst Daniele Pampaloni and the team at Tap Grafiche quietly got on with printing the book.

Putting a lifetime's photos together with a biography was a project always in doubt. I just wanted to do it. Judge for yourself if it should have been two books. There are more where this came from if you ask!

web@stephenpearce.com

CLOSER

I wrote this book now, before I forgot it all. I never asked my parents about their lives. In case my children don't ask me, here are the nuts and bolts. To tell all would take forever so this is a taste. This book is dedicated to everyone everywhere. May your journey be a rewarding one. For me it has all been made more worthwhile by having the nose to choose a great traveling companion: Lauren. Both she and my former wife Francesca have created an amazing next generation: Lucy, Mirin, Oran. If my father, mother and I and Lauren and her parents were independent souls, our three musketeers are way, way out there. Keep on flying guys.

Having just read the acknowledgements in my daughter Lucy's book *Moon Time* it seemed to me that the women in our family carry the wisdom, quietly getting on with it. My grandmother, mother, daughters Lucy and Mirin and my wife Lauren.

Then I looked at myself and realised that I also carry wisdom, and so does my son Oran. The wisdom of our family and the wisdom of the universe. I have always been quite careful to hide my wisdom with tomfoolery. I have thought wisdom to be boring, like unwanted advice and I have always wanted to be cooler than that! I have wanted to write but felt that nobody would want to read what I really want to say as it is mostly against the flow of common wisdom, or stupidity as I see it. I see most of the thrust of mans' efforts as ignorance and stupidity which will probably leave the earth spinning happily without us!

My feeling of not wanting to risk saying what I feel is so strong that I suspect that in another life I did, and paid the ultimate price and so don't want to go through all of that pain again. Burning at a stake or being stoned to death is no joke.

S☺P

Still in love. Photo Michael MacSweeney 2012.

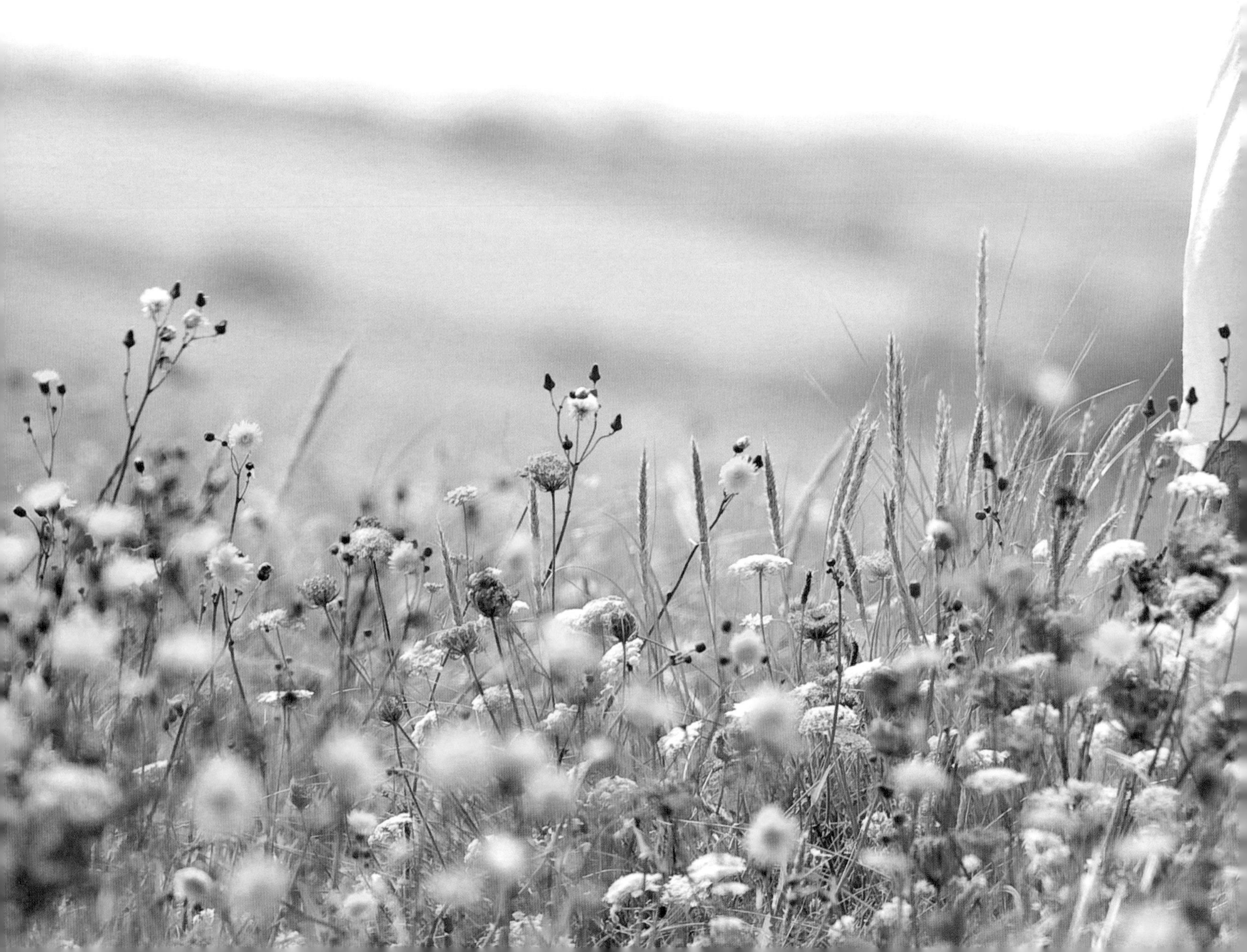

RESERVED
for your comments and children's drawings